Precision and Depth

IN FLANNERY O'CONNOR'S SHORT STORIES

T0107995

Karl-Heinz Westarp

Precision and Depth

IN FLANNERY O'CONNOR'S SHORT STORIES

AARHUS UNIVERSITY PRESS

2002

Precision and Depth
in Flannery O'Connor's Short Stories
is printed by Narayana Press, Denmark
© Karl-Heinz Westarp and Aarhus University Press 2002
Cover by Jørgen Sparre with drawing of Flannery O'Connor
by Dan Nemteanu, 1992
Printed in Denmark 2002

ISBN 87 7288 937 3

Published with the financial support of
The Danish Research Council for the Humanities and
Aarhus University Research Foundation

Aarhus University Press
Langelandsgade 177
DK-8200 Aarhus N
Phone (+45) 8942 5370
Fax (+45) 8942 5380

73 Lime Walk
Headington, Oxford OX3 7AD
Fax (+44) 1865 750 079

Box 511
oakville, Connecticut 06779
Fax (+1) 860 945 9468

www.unipress.dk

For my patient wife Jette
and our helpful children
Filip, Kamilla and Samuel

Table of Contents

Chapter 1

Precision and Depth in Flannery O'Connor's Short Stories:

A SUMMARIZING INTRODUCTION

Singular & Particular Detail is the Foundation of the Sublime.
WILLIAM BLAKE

Bishop Lancelot Andrewes takes a word and derives the world from it; squeezing and squeezing the word until it yields a full juice of meaning which we should never have supposed any word to possess. In this process the qualities, … of ordonnance and precision, are exercised.
T.S. ELIOT

Flannery O'Connor, I contend, combined Blake's insistence on the particular with the precise word for the sake of depth in meaning that Eliot found in Lancelot Andrewes. 'Symbols', O'Connor states, 'are details that, while having their essential place in the literal level of the story, operate in depth as well as on the surface, increasing the story in every direction' (MM 71) and symbols 'should go on deepening' (CW 924). One of my aims with the different parts of this study is to analyze O'Connor's reasons for her insistence on the necessary interconnection between surface precision and depth. I consider metaphor, 'the ever-present, ever-varying conjunction of the known and unknown',[1] as a crucial key to a comprehensive understanding of O'Connor's work.

All language is in the widest sense of the word metaphorical, because whatever signification a word contains this has been 'carried over' (the Greek word for that is 'meta-phérein') from one form of existence to another, a phenomenon in the real world – physical or mental – has become a linguistic phenomenon, which can be used for communication processes between humans. If the linguistic phenomenon is not precise,

---

1 This is Edward Kessler's definition in *Flannery O'Connor and the Language of Apocalypse*, Princeton University Press, 1986, 12.

communication is made difficult or – in the extreme – impossible. Linguistic precision is therefore a *non-plus-ultra* for the artist who creates new worlds with words.

According to Jewish/Christian mythology the world came into being through the word of the Creator in an original metaphoric process: the eternal Spirit setting a world that is other than pure spirit. The creation of the world as the concretized image of the Creator or the created world as an 'enfleshing' or 'incarnation' of the Creator. Therefore every form of being in the created world partakes in the spirit and is therefore diaphanous to an underlying 'depth dimension'.

In the fullness of time the eternal Word – the Logos – of the Creator was – according to the Christian faith – 'enfleshed', 'incarnated' in a human called Jesus. As the Gospel according to John formulates it (1:14) 'The Word became flesh' (Logos sarx egéneto, Verbum caro factum est), spiritual reality became concrete, through the senses perceivable reality. The incarnated Logos was in this world with the single purpose to bring the offer of rebirth in the spirit by the grace of the Creator to all humans blinded and fettered by the bondage of fallen flesh. Thus the incarnated Logos, the enfleshed Word, brings word of good news, good tidings of redemption, *Word of God in Words of Men*.[2]

Metaphoricity works in two diametrically opposed ways in theology, as well as in language and in poetic creation: in the first direction motion goes from spiritual to physical reality, the second movement goes into the opposite direction in that the physical reality points to, becomes translucent to an underlying spiritual reality. This means in the realm of theology that God's spirit is concretized in the creation, the Logos is enfleshed in Jesus, a process theologians call 'descending Christology';[3] similarly in language analysis according to Saussure the mental signifier/signified is concretized in the linguistic sign or the word; and poetic inspiration takes the form of a text. Metaphoricity in the opposite direction is in theology the search for the divine in created nature,[4] for the 'inscape of things' as Gerard Manley Hopkins called this

---

2   The title of a book by Jean Levie on *The Bible, Word of God in Words of Men*, which O'Connor reviewed in *The Southern Cross* on March 2, 1963.

3   Philippians 2:6-7 'Though he was in the form of God, ... he emptied himself, ... being born in the likeness of men'.

4   Romans 1:20 'Ever since the creation of the world his invisible nature, namely, his eternal power and deity, has been clearly perceived in the things that have been made'.

search, and the detection of Christ's divinity in the man Jesus, the 'mediator' between God and man, who was 'exalted',[5] what theologians call 'ascending Christology', to bring the spirit of grace to mankind through word and deed. In language analysis this means that a word 'makes sense', has a meaning in the communicative process. Finally in poetry the second direction of metaphoricity means that the text with its concrete words and images is pried open in the hermeneutic process to reveal its multi-layered and polyvalent meanings, the concrete word becomes epiphanic, to use James Joyce's term, or as Flannery O'Connor formulated it: 'The longer you look at one object [here: word], the more of the world you see in it' (MM 77).

To see these three areas of two-way metaphoricity with their many parallels as one was, I hope to show, Flannery O'Connor's ambitious poetic project. Therefore she was such a perfectionist in her attempt to find precise and concrete words and images, for only thus, she was convinced, could she guarantee the depth dimension which could shock her reader into new awareness about the meaning of life. As she wrote to Eileen Hall in 1956: 'Art is not anything that goes on "among" people, not the art of the novel anyway. It is something that one experiences alone and for the purpose of realizing in a fresh way, through the senses, the mystery of existence' (CW 988).

WORD MADE FLESH MADE WORD: THEOLOGICAL METAPHORICITY

For O'Connor, the artist, knowledge about the fundamental tenets of Christian faith was a necessity and a lived reality. The books in her library, her letters and her book reviews amply prove the seriousness she dedicated to the study of Christian thought. Centrally placed is her interest in the Incarnation and she called fiction 'so very much an incarnational art' (MM 68). In 1955 she wrote in a letter to her friend 'A':[6] 'One of the awful things about writing when you are a Christian is that

---

5   Philippians 2:9 'Therefore God has highly exalted him'.

6   The identity of 'A' as Betty Hester, with whom O'Connor carried on an intensive correspondence ever since her first letter on July 20th 1955 (HB 90), was revealed to me in an e-mail of February 1st, 1999 by William Sessions, another of O'Connor's and 'A''s friends (HB 145). He wrote: 'My friend Betty Hester shot herself the day after Christmas [1998]'.

for you the ultimate reality is the Incarnation, the present reality is the Incarnation, the whole reality is the Incarnation, and nobody believes in the Incarnation; that is, nobody in the audience. My audience are the people who think God is dead. At least these are the people I am conscious of writing for' (CW 943).[7] O'Connor mentions the Church's emphasis on the body[8] and says that 'the fact of the Word made flesh ... is the fulcrum that lifts my particular stories'.[9] God's creation of enfleshing and thus uniting spirit in matter[10] reached for her its peak in the Incarnation. Here O'Connor proves to be in keeping not only with biblical thinking but also with major theologians. Hebrews 11:3 reads: 'By faith we understand that the world was created by the word of God, so that what is seen was made out of things which do not appear'. This understanding of the creation is also that of Thomas Aquinas[11] according to whom 'das innergöttliche Wort der Ursprung der geschaffenen Wesen ist'.[12] The same theological thinking is found in Raphael Schultz who says that God's creative act 'ist geschehen *durch* das eine vollkommene *Wort Gottes*, in dem Gott als Urheber alles Seins und Lebens sich selbst als in einem Anderen so vollkommen ausspricht'.[13] In keeping with this understanding of the creation O'Connor in her review of Karl Barth's book *Evangelical Theology: An Introduction* made Barth's definition of theology her own: it 'is science seeking the knowledge of the Word of God in God's work'.[14] This work is brought to completion in Jesus, 'born in the likeness of men', in whom 'God's active power embodied itself in a visible man'.[15] The Gospel according to John formu-

---

7 Richard Giannone sums up O'Connor's attitude: 'A disincarnate faith offends O'Connor'. 'Warfare and Solitude: O'Connor's Prophet and the Word in the Desert'. Murphy, John J. et al. eds, *Flannery O'Connor and the Christian Mystery*, Salt Lake City, 1997, 184.

8 See letter to 'A', HB 100.

9 Letter to C. Dawkins, HB 227.

10 O'Connor attacked the Manicheans because they 'separated spirit and matter' (MM 68).

11 O'Connor had read his *Summa* 'for about twenty minutes every night' (HB 93).

12 This formulation is H. Krings's in 'Wort' I. Philosophisch. *Handbuch theologischer Grundbegriffe* Band 4, DTV, München, 1962, 425.

13 Schultz, Raphael, 'Sakrament'. Rahner, Karl et al. eds, *Sacramentum Mundi*, Herder, Freiburg 1968, vol. 4, 338.

14 Reprinted in Lorine M. Getz, ed., *Flannery O'Connor, Literary Theologian*, Edwin Mellen Press, Lewiston, 1999, 203.

15 Price, Reynolds, 'The Gospel According to Saint John'. Corn, Alfred, ed., *Incarnation: Contemporary Writers on the New Testament*, Viking, NY, 1990, 43. Corn, who was also one of O'Connor's correspondents (HB 476), dedicated his book among others to Flannery O'Connor.

lates this in its prologue at 1:14: 'And the Word became flesh and dwelt among us'. Karl Rahner, with whose theology O'Connor was familiar,[16] defines the incarnated Logos[17] as 'die höchste Selbstmitteilung Gottes' in which 'Gott sich selbst der *Welt* zusagt' and where Christ 'ist nicht nur ein möglicher Mitteiler eines Heils ... sondern ist diese Mitteilung als unwiderrufliche und geschichtlich erscheinende selbst' which is 'der Höhepunkt und das Zentrum der Vergöttlichung der Welt'.[18] In these few words Rahner formulates what became known as 'descending Christology' or the *kenosis* (Philippians 2:7) of God's Word, which becomes an integral part of the world, and 'ascending Christology',[19] the *hypsoma* (Philippians 2:9) or the exaltation of God's humble servant and with it the 'deification' of the world through God's grace.[20] 'When spirit penetrates matter, the infinite *I AM* becomes the integer *IS* and transforms the world: "The Word made flesh has returned to the world its full dimensions."[21][22] This is how Emily Archer and Frederick Asals formulate the incarnational process and its results, which characterize O'Connor's works. As I see it O'Connor became through her work what Teilhard de Chardin had asked for in *The Divine Milieu*, a Catholic who is 'passionately vowed by conviction and not by convention to spreading the hopes of the Incarnation'.[23]

The enfleshed 'word of God is living and active' (Hebrews 4:12) and 'kommt im Wort der Apostel zur Aussage'.[24] The enfleshed word becomes word again in the good tidings or the 'gospel', *The Bible, Word of God in Words of Men*, which is why Augustine thinks of the Incarnation

16 She had read Rahner's *The Theology of Death* (HB 520).

17 Giannone Anglicizes 'incarnated' as 'enfleshed', l.c. 177.

18 'Inkarnation'. Rahner, Karl et al. eds, *Sacramentum Mundi*, Herder, Freiburg, 1968, vol. 2, 825; 839.

19 To Kilcourse O'Connor's work is characterized by her 'belief in an "ascending christology."' Kilcourse, George, '"Parker's Back": "Not Totally Congenial" Icons of Christ'. Murphy, John J. et al. eds, *Flannery O'Connor and the Christian Mystery*, Salt Lake City, 1997, 36.

20 Cp. 1 John 3:1: 'See what love the Father has given us, that we should be called children of God; and so we are'.

21 Asals, Frederick, *Flannery O'Connor: The Imagination of Extremity*, Athens, University of Georgia Press, 1982, 72.

22 Archer, Emily, 'Naming in the Neighborhood of Being: O'Connor and Percy on Language'. *Studies in the Literary Imagination*, vol. 20 no 2 (1987) 108.

23 O'Connor quoted this passage in her 1961 review of Teilhard's book *The Divine Milieu*, reprinted in Getz, op.cit., 162.

24 Scheffczyk, Leo, 'Wort Gottes'. Rahner, Karl et al. eds, *Sacramentum Mundi*, Herder, Freiburg, 1968, vol. 4, 1404.

as an 'inverbation' where 'das Wort Gottes als bleibende Heilskraft anerkannt [wird]'.[25] For O'Connor the sacraments were the most prominent incarnational signs of the power of God's sanctifying grace.[26] Here physical signs – such as water in baptism – accompanied by words[27] bring about the redemption of the person baptized.[28] O'Connor is looking for such 'pregnant' signs in the concrete world in which the depth of ultimate reality can radiate. But since she is aware of the fact that she writes for an audience who think God is dead and who do not believe in the Incarnation, she has to define 'something by defining what it is not'.[29] Here lies the reason for O'Connor's 'grotesque' situations, her freaks, her modern metaphysical conceits. According to Emily Archer O'Connor's is 'a sacramental world', in which 'groomed pigs, idiot children, and peacocks all have the capacity to "pant with a secret life" [CS 508]'.[30] It was therefore essential for O'Connor to draw her friends' and readers' attention to the quadruple way of reading a text, the literal, the allegorical, the moral and the anagogical,[31] of which the last was most important for her 'double vision' as Frederick Asals calls O'Connor's sacramentalism.[32] In 'The Nature and Aim of Fiction' she says: 'The kind of vision the fiction writer needs to have, or to develop, in order to increase the meaning of his story is called anagogical vision, and that is the kind of vision that is able to see different levels of reality in one image or one situation. ... anagogical [has] to do with the

---

25 Ibid. 1406.
26 Whenever she could O'Connor participated in the Eucharist and in *The Violent Bear It Away* she dramatized the baptism of the idiot child Bishop.
27 Matthew 28:19: 'Baptizing them in the name of the Father and of the Son and of the Holy Spirit'.
28 Raphael Schultz defines a 'sacrament' as follows: 'Ihrem Wesen nach sind die Sakramente ... aus "Materie" (...res) und "Form" (Wort) zusammengesetzte "sichtbare" Zeichen oder Symbole der "unsichtbaren" Gnade'. L.c. 330.
29 Angle, Kimberly Greene, 'Flannery O'Connor's Literary Art: Spiritual Portraits in Negative Space'. *The Flannery O'Connor Bulletin*, vol. 23 (1994-95) 160. Angle's 'negative-space theory' is a modern reformulation of Aquinas' *via negativa*.
30 Op.cit. 101.
31 She mentions these levels of medieval Scripture reading in a letter of March 13, 1962 to Charlotte Gafford (HB 468-69) and in 'The Nature and Aim of Fiction' (MM 72).
32 Op.cit. 79. Joyce Carol Oates acknowledges influence from O'Connor on her own double vision: 'Le monde naturel ordinaire est soit sacramental (et cérémoniel) soit profane (et vulgaire). Et donc, le corps malade est non seulement l'expression, ou l'intensification symbolique, de la "maladie" spirituelle qui accompagne les processus physiques'. 'L'Imagination de Flannery O'Connor'. *Europe-Revue Littéraire Mensuelle* 75.816 (1997) 44.

Divine life and our participation in it' (MM 72). 'To see straight' (HB 131), to look at the concrete reality of the world 'in order to find at its depths the image of its source, the image of ultimate reality' (MM 157) was according to Archer[33] O'Connor's synonym for the anagogical vision. Horton Davies[34] and Edward Kessler[35] have drawn attention to a number of anagogical signals in O'Connor's works. 'The first and most common theological pointer or anagogical signal is *incompleteness*. It points to the reality of original sin, the defect in the human being in need of grace for salvation',[36] in other words O'Connor's focus on our post-lapsarian status.[37] The second anagogical pointer is her use of *eyes*,[38] the third *the red orb of the setting sun*, which 'presence in the sky is the moment of judgment and grace'.[39] The fourth signal is the use of *liturgical colors*, where 'purple has a ... premonitory significance, ... for it is sometimes mentioned immediately prior to the decision that brings grace or spiritual enlightenment in a story'.[40] The fifth signal is the use of *'as if'*, which Kessler deals with in greater detail than Davies and the importance of which I shall return to in the following discussion of some linguistic aspects of metaphoricity.

LINGUISTIC POINTERS OF METAPHORICITY

Irwin Howard Streight has called O'Connor's language 'incarnational'[41] and Max Edelman Boren thinks that 'if there is a key to understanding her writing, it is through the "word made flesh." ... The Incarnation is

---

33 Op.cit. 102.

34 Davies, Horton, 'Anagogical Signs in Flannery O'Connor's Fiction'. *Thought*, vol. 55 (1980), 428-38.

35 Op.cit., especially 51-73.

36 Davies, ibid. 430.

37 In her letter of May 4, 1963 to Sr. Gable O'Connor wrote 'The writer has to make the corruption believable before he can make the grace meaningful' (HB 516).

38 'For the writer of fiction, everything has its testing point in the eye, an organ which eventually involves the whole personality and as much of the world as can be got into it' O'Connor wrote (MM 144).

39 Ibid. 434. I have dealt with this signal in extenso in 'Flannery O'Connor's Translucent Settings', *American Studies in Scandinavia*, vol. 31, no 2 (1999), 31-41. See also chapter III below.

40 Ibid. 436.

41 'A Good Hypogram Is Not Hard to Find'. Murphy, John J. et al. eds, *Flannery O'Connor and the Christian Mystery*, Salt Lake City, 1997, 233.

used by O'Connor as a literary device for rendering profound significance; she finds the divine in material, physical language. ... It is a material, fleshy language, deformed and mutating, that creates a "texture of existence"' and 'a unique text as deeply profound as it is concrete'.[42] O'Connor was fully aware of the detrimental impact that her religious upbringing might have upon her prose and therefore she tried 'militantly never to be affected by the pious language of the faithful' (CW 944).[43] For her work as a writer had to start 'where all human knowledge begins – with the senses' (MM 155). The senses transfer impressions of the concrete – 'inspired' – world, to the human brain, where they are linked with words which, according to John Locke, are 'sensible marks of ideas, and the ideas they stand for are their proper and immediate signification'.[44] Words must be concrete and precise, otherwise they cannot be 'translucent, with shadowed depths beyond each word'.[45] Critics have used a number of epithets to characterize O'Connor's prose. It is 'pellucid, controlled, and unadventurous'[46] and Melody Graulich calls it 'concrete, earthy, ironic language, so unlike the ethereal, high-minded, abstract diction commonly associated with religious writers. Her language is O'Connor's strength. ... Through distortion, indirection, "gaps," negations, and ambiguous language, O'Connor finds the way'.[47] Fred Chappell bases O'Connor's intensity of presentation upon a 'phalanx of tartly precise detail, [a] perfect-pitch reporting of dialogue'.[48]

O'Connor herself was aware of literary predecessors who had used language for revelatory purposes,[49] such as Joyce, who called 'a sudden

---

42 'Flannery O'Connor, laughter and the Word made flesh'. *Studies in American Fiction*, vol. 26 no 1 (1998) 124, 126.

43 Part of the 'caricature of Christianity' that she thought also had oppressed Teilhard de Chardin's early years. Getz, op.cit. 149.

44 'Essay Concerning Human Understanding', Book 3 chapt. II.1, quoted in Selden, Raman, ed., *The Theory of Criticism*, Longman, London, 1988, 108.

45 Betts, Doris, 'Talking to Flannery'. Gordon, Sarah, ed., *Flannery O'Connor: In Celebration of Genius*, Athens, Ga.: Hill Street Press, 2000, 112.

46 Bawer, Bruce, 'Under the Aspect of Eternity: The Fiction of Flannery O'Connor', *The Aspect of Eternity*, Greywolf Press, Saint Paul, 1993, 320.

47 '"They Ain't Nothing but Words": Flannery O'Connor's *Wise Blood*. *The Flannery O'Connor Bulletin*, vol. 7 (1978) 83.

48 'Vertigo'. Gordon, Sarah, ed., *Flannery O'Connor: In Celebration of Genius*, Athens, Ga.: Hill Street Press, 2000, 27.

49 Kessler thinks that 'O'Connor and Eliot create metaphors of displacement or estrangement that make way for the "revelation" of a new world'. Op.cit. 20.

spiritual manifestation, whether in the vulgarity of speech or of gesture'
an epiphany[50] which in a typically paradoxical O'Connor formulation
'may be a matter of recognizing the Holy Ghost in fiction by the way
he chooses to conceal himself' (HB 130). She was also familiar with
Gerard Manley Hopkins' concept of 'inscape' (HB 517). According to
Marion Montgomery 'from the witness of her letters, one sees that the
whole world shines for her with that presence which Gerard Manley
Hopkins pursues as the inscape of the particular, discrete creatures of
this world'.[51] It seems to me that Hopkins' inscape covers precisely the
way in which O'Connor sees reality and uses words to describe it. 'In
Hopkins' celebration of the sensuous, the concrete, the particular – his
"instress of the inscapes" [both of things and of words] – all of these
[motifs] converge. As a Catholic, Hopkins was an incarnationist and a
sacramentalist: the sacraments are the extensions of the Incarnation. ...
"Inscape" stands for any kind of formed or focused view, any pattern
discerned in the natural world. A central word in his vocabulary and
central motif in his mental life, it traverses some range of meaning: from
sense-perceived pattern to inner form. The prefix seems to imply a contrary, an outerscape: that is, an "inscape" is not mechanically or inertly
present but requires personal action, attention, a seeing and a seeing
into'.[52] The concept that O'Connor herself uses for the translucency of
her prose is 'radiance' which seems to combine Joyce's epiphany and
Hopkins' inscape. In her essay 'Catholic Novelists and Their Readers'
she states: Writers should pay 'strict attention to the order, proportion,
and radiance of what they are making' (MM 189). Or as she writes in
'A Good Man Is Hard to Find': 'The trees were full of silver-white sun-
light and the meanest of them sparkled' (CS 119).[53]

There are two more linguistically oriented approaches to an understanding of O'Connor's metaphoricity. The French semiotician Michael
Riffaterre has coined the sociolinguistic concept of the *hypogram* – lit-
erally 'that which is written underneath' – which Irwin Howard
Streight has successfully applied to an analysis O'Connor's prose. Riffaterre calls his model 'hypogrammatical because a deictic sign points to

---

50 Joyce, James, *Stephen Hero*, New Directions, New York, 1963, 211.

51 *Why Flannery O'Connor Stayed Home*, Sherwood Sugden, La Salle, Ill., 1981, 459.

52 Warren, Austin, 'Instress of Inscape' in Geoffrey H. Hartman, ed., *Hopkins*, Prentice-
Hall, Englewood Cliffs, 1966, 168; 171.

53 This radiant light characterizes the transfigured Jesus on the mountain, Mark 9:2-3:
'his garments became glistening, intensely white'.

a latent text, to a hypogram underneath the text, ... and from this the text draws its significance'.[54] In his article 'A Good Hypogram Is Not Hard to Find' Streight copiously exemplifies how the concept of the hypogram can illuminate O'Connor's metaphoric language. 'A hypogram is an absent presence; in a sacral sense, it allows for and effects the generative force of the Word upon the word. For O'Connor, who I contend uses language "incarnationally," the hypogram abides in the heaven of the "added dimension" (MM 150) that she spoke of as being manifest in her stories, from which the Word/word as Logos (meaning) has come down to the lexical and semantic terrain of the text'. For example 'the animated sun is a signal for the O'Connor reader that some epiphanic encounter is about to take place'.[55]

The other is O'Connor's frequent use of the copula *as if*. Edward Kessler has, as mentioned above, drawn attention to its importance as an anagogical pointer in O'Connor's fiction. He adduces a number of examples where he sees a metaphoric duplicity in this feature. The particle *as* characteristic of the simile expresses a similarity between tenor and vehicle, whereas the *as if* undermines this similarity. Kessler says that 'metaphor as lie – the bringing together of two incongruous entities *as if* they were one – remains the poet's only means of pointing toward the true. ... O'Connor's *as if* copula ... signals that mere resemblance ... cannot bring about radical change in how we see. Simile can intensify our awareness of the given world, but it does not, like O'Connor's *as if*, yoke together unambiguous declarative sentences with metaphoric uncertainty'.[56] 'The *as if* offers imaginative access to the unknown, a bridge between veristic resemblances and the ultimate substance of all O'Connor's fiction: apocalyptic power, that which for convenience we call mystery'.[57]

No matter which of the above approaches we use or which concept we apply in an attempt to get to grips with O'Connor's linguistic metaphoricity, all of them make it clear that in her prose she presents a surface reality characterized by precision of detail, which is enjoyable in it-

---

54 'Hermeneutic Models'. *Poetry Today* vol. 4.1 (1983) 13. Cp. Hilton Als, who in 'The Lonesome Place: Flannery O'Connor on race and religion in the unreconstructed South'. *The New Yorker* January 29, 2001, 84 states that 'O'Connor preferred stories that were direct in their telling and mysterious only in their subtext'.

55 In Murphy, John J. et al. eds, *Flannery O'Connor and the Christian Mystery*, Salt Lake City, 1997, 233.

56 Op.cit. 9, 21.

57 Ibid. 111.

self because of its artistic perfection, but that this surface invites the reader to look beyond. As Kessler has formulated it: 'O'Connor's metaphors consistently do two things, with a minimum of strain: intensifying our awareness of creating nature while, through the "darkness of parable," opening up a way beyond the world, a "presence" external to words'.[58]

DEPTH *THROUGH* PRECISION: ART AS METAPHOR

In the following presentation of O'Connor's view upon the artist, art and her way of performing and perfecting her art I shall try to show that awareness of metaphoricity, of the metadiscourse enfleshed in the surface discourse of the text is always present.

The short biographical note which follows further down and my published material document O'Connor's life as an artist. Suffice it therefore here to say that for O'Connor the vocation of the artist demanded fulltime dedication and that she was fully aware of the artist's special obligation. 'The writer is one who operates at a peculiar crossroads where time and place and eternity somehow meet. [The writer's] problem is to find that location' (MM 59).[59] Already in this characterization it is clear that O'Connor knew she had to be fully aware of the concrete life experiences which in themselves contain the depth dimension of otherness. She described herself as having 'one of those food-chopper brains that nothing comes out of the way it went in'.[60] 'I suppose the fullest writing comes from what has been accepted and experienced both. ... Conviction without experience makes for harshness' (CW 949). She was convinced that the artist had to be at one with the created world in order to be able to reveal the creator behind it. 'It is mainly due to the artist's adherence to the visible that he is able to reveal the invisible; the artist has to accept limitations in order to transcend them'.[61] And she admonished herself: 'The artist himself always has to

---

58 Ibid. 15.

59 Meena Alexander, a writer with a multiethnic background has said: 'The act of writing was also for me an act of translating across zones'. 'The Postcolonial Imagination', interview with Prem Poddar. *Himal – South Asian*, vol. 14 no 1, (2001) 14.

60 Letter February 13, 1954 to Ben Griffith, CW 918. O'Connor's formulation is reminiscent of Coleridge's definition of artistic imagination: 'It dissolves, dissipates, in order to re-create'. *Biographia Literaria* chapter 13, quoted in Selden, op.cit. 145.

remember that what he is rearranging *is* nature, and that he has to know it and be able to describe it accurately in order to have the authority to rearrange it all' (MM 98).[62] The constant awareness of the duplicity of purpose in writing was important for O'Connor: precision in the description of nature, but always also stressing the fact that 'the main purpose of the fiction writer is with mystery as it is incarnated in human life' (MM 176) together with the obligation never to overstep one's limits as an artist.[63] O'Connor's multiple concerns as an artist are summed up by Marion Montgomery: she had to pay 'strict attention to a multiple burden as artist, to the tedious labor of words and to the limitation of human understanding in the presence of mystery'.[64]

For O'Connor the art work was not only demanding for the writer. If s/he had enfleshed a vision properly, the perception of the work was also a continuously exerting experience for the reader. 'A story is good when you continue to see more and more in it, and when it continues to escape you. In fiction two and two is always more than four' (MM 102). What is true for the artist, i.e. that s/he needs to pay attention to precision and detail in experience and the expression thereof, is also true for the reader who has to pay careful attention to all the details of the text, though he will never get to 'the end'. The reader must understand that 'fiction must always be an incarnational art, and as such it must work completely by analogy,[65] through outward signs of the inward'.[66] Miller Williams reports O'Connor having said that she was always looking for 'the truth, but understand that it is not necessarily what happened'[67] and to her friend 'A' O'Connor wrote that 'it is the business of the artist to uncover the strangeness of truth' (CW 1101).

---

61 Bieber, Christina, 'Called to the Beautiful: The Incarnational Art of Flannery O'Connor's *The Violent Bear It Away*. *Xavier Review* vol. 18 no 1 (1998) 56.

62 As Paul LaCroix had said: 'Naturen er kun en ordbog, hvoraf kunstneren skaber værket'. Quoted by Dan Ringgaard in his Chicago SASS lecture on April 27, 2001.

63 'What-is is all [the writer] has to do with; the concrete is his medium; and he will realize eventually that fiction can transcend its limitations only by staying within them' (MM 146).

64 Op.cit. 59.

65 O'Connor had told Miller Williams that 'every good story is a parable'. 'Remembering Flannery O'Connor'. Gordon, Sarah, ed., *Flannery O'Connor: In Celebration of Genius*, Athens, Ga.: Hill Street Press, 2000, 3.

66 Fickett, Harold, and Douglas R. Gilbert, *Flannery O'Connor: Images of Grace*, Grand Rapids, Mi, Eerdmans, 1986, 49.

67 L.c.

In order to elevate art to its incarnational status O'Connor knew that she would have to pay careful attention to concrete sense impressions, to translate them into precise wording, to use unfamiliar or even distorted images to lead the reader *through* manners to the experience of the depth dimension of mystery. She knew that fiction 'operates through the senses. ... No reader who doesn't actually experience, who isn't made feel the story is going to believe anything the fiction writer merely tells him' (MM 91). The 'concrete details of life ... make actual the mystery of our position on earth' (MM 68). 'Whatever the novelist sees in the way of truth must first take on the form of his art and must become embodied in the concrete and human. ... every mystery that reaches the human mind ... does so by way of the senses' (MM 175). 'Weltanschauung'[68] started for O'Connor with sense impressions, and she considered that as being of special importance to the artist. When she spoke to young writers she always admonished them to start with the rendering of sense impressions and stay away from abstractions or mere telling. 'The beginning of human knowledge is through the senses, and the fiction writer begins where human perception begins. He appeals through the senses, and you cannot appeal to the senses with abstractions. ... the world of the fiction writer is full of matter, and this is what the beginning fiction writers are very loath to create. They are concerned primarily with unfleshed ideas and emotions' (MM 67). She considered it a major part of her task as a novelist 'to make everything, even an ultimate concern, as solid, as concrete, as specific as possible' (MM 155) and 'to portray reality as it manifests itself in our concrete, sensual life' (MM 170). As much as she herself was willing to ask friends to read her work and advise her, was she concerned to help her writer friends on the way. To Ben Griffith she wrote in 1955: 'You have got to learn to paint with words.[69] ... The old man [in your novel] thinks of the daughter-in-law and son talking and recalls their conversation – well he should see them, the reader should see them, should feel from seeing them what their conversation is going to be almost before he hears it' (CW 938).

---

68 Schleiermacher, who coined this concept, defined it as 'to see, to cognize the universe in its sensuous detail'. (Quoted in Selden, R., op.cit. 199.)

69 In Chapter III below I discuss the importance of O'Connor's own painting for her writing process. Joyce Carol Oates said of O'Connor: 'Son imagination était visuelle et littérale'. L.c. 46.

For O'Connor art was necessarily realist art, because 'the artist penetrates the concrete world in order to find at its depths the image of its source, the image of ultimate reality' (MM 157). Throughout her career O'Connor was an adamant reader, always concerned about improving her art. She admired other authors for their perfection in literary performance. About a scene in her friend Caroline Gordon Tate's short story 'Summer Dust' she wrote to 'A': 'She is ... great on getting things there so concretely that they can't possibly escape – note how that horse goes through that gate, the sun on the neck and then on the girl's leg and then she turns and watches it slide off his rump. That is real masterly doing, and nobody does it any better than Caroline' (HB 149). She had met Katherine Anne Porter and knew about the problems she had with finishing her novel[70] but she was also aware that what she did have 'aplenty is the ability to make things actual. [She] can create the sweating stinking life out of anything, the purely animal' (HB 481). Making things actual was also what O'Connor admired in Joyce, especially his rendering of the snow in 'The Dead'. She wrote Ben Griffith: 'See how he makes the snow work in that story. Chekhov makes everything work – the air, the light, the cold, the dirt etc'. (HB 84) Andrea Hollander Budy, who admired O'Connor's 'ability to envision, to locate her stories, detail by detail, and to deliver her characters *through* those details', comments that O'Connor was in a constant learning process to improve her work that 'its language must be alert, its images fresh and honest, and its concise particulars, which may seem almost accidentally included, must deliver – with a chill of recognition – the enduring world'.[71] Marion Montgomery, another fellow Georgian writer, used the following image for O'Connor's precision in language: 'This Georgia poet has an eye for detail, out of which she builds metaphor that is as close to earth as Saint Teresa in the kitchen'.[72] O'Connor also admired Conrad whose 'aim as an artist was to render the highest possible justice to the visible universe'. She adds about her own art that 'for me the visible universe is a reflection of the invisible universe' (HB 128).

The sheer physicality of language was of paramount importance to O'Connor because 'it should reinforce our sense of the supernatural by grounding it in concrete, observable reality' (MM 148). She was an-

---

70 *Ship of Fools*, 1962.
71 'An Enduring Chill'. Gordon, Sarah, ed., *Flannery O'Connor: In Celebration of Genius*, Athens, Ga.: Hill Street Press, 2000, 70.
72 Op.cit. 11.

noyed when critics blamed her for her shockingly concrete pictures, which were thought to be 'perverse'. She defended herself by stating: 'Isn't it arbitrary to call these images such as the cat-faced baby and the old woman that looked like a cedar fence post and the grandfather who went around with Jesus hidden in his head like a stinger – perverse? They are right, accurate, so why perverse?' (HB 470) In a world where the author has to shout to the deaf and draw startling pictures for the blind of depth-perception she was convinced she had to resort to unconventional and distorted images that 'connect or combine or embody two points; one is a point in the concrete, and the other is a point not visible to the naked eye, but believed in by him firmly' (MM 42). In her desire to reach out to the reader and make him see she chose extreme formulations but she also used clichés in new ways. She used distortion or the negative sides of human behavior and character as 'the only way to make people see' (CW 932).[73] In her search for concrete images in her stories O'Connor did not shy away from the use of violence. She found 'that violence is strangely capable of returning my characters to reality and preparing them to accept their moment of grace' (MM 112). 'Grace, to the Catholic way of thinking, can and does use as its medium the imperfect, purely human, and even hypocritical' (HB 389). Criticism has now come around to seeing her use of violence no longer as 'gratuitous ... it is essential as a device to move the reader toward something else, something that could be seen as the embodiment of the story's mystery'.[74]

As a poet O'Connor had detected a kindred intelligence in Teilhard de Chardin. In her review of his book *The Phenomenon of Man* she wrote: 'His is a scientific expression of what the poet attempts to do: penetrate matter until spirit is revealed in it'.[75] It was her prime aim as a fiction writer to present mystery 'as it is incarnated in human life'

---

73 In her Chicago SASS lecture on the concept of 'svimmelhed' in Kierkegaard's works (April 27, 2001) Pia Søltoft said that Kierkegaard with this concept describes 'fænomenets vrangside og herigennem erfaring af det sublime', which seems to me a striking parallel to O'Connor's depiction of her characters as 'loathsome beasts'. (Allen, William Rodney, 'The Cage of Matter: The World as Zoo in Flannery O'Connor's *Wise Blood*. *American Literature: A Journal of Literary History, Criticism, and Bibliography*, vol. 58 no 2 (1986) 259.) O'Connor had read Kierkegaard's *Fear and Trembling* (HB 273).

74 Whitt, Margaret Earley, *Flannery O'Connor*, University of South Carolina Press, Columbia, 1997, 11.

75 Getz, op.cit. 180.

(MM 176), in concrete situations. What the writer 'sees on the surface will be of interest to him only as he can go through it into an experience of mystery itself. ... Such a writer will be interested in what we don't understand rather than in what we do' (CW 816; MM 41-42).[76] O'Connor has given us a number of striking examples of images, which are entirely plausible on the surface level and continue to be so while at the same time they take on a constantly growing depth dimension, which renders them unforgettable. A sign, according to Longinus, of true greatness in literature which 'gives abundant food for thought: it is irksome, nay, impossible, to resist its effect: the memory of it is stubborn and indelible'.[77] An example of this is Haze, O'Connor's protagonist in *Wise Blood*, who looking up saw that 'the black sky was underpinned with long silver streaks that looked like scaffolding and depth upon depth behind it were thousands of stars that all seemed to be moving very slowly as if they were about some vast construction work that involved the whole order of the universe and would take all time to complete'. And later again 'the entire distance that extended from his eyes to the blank sky that went on, depth after depth, into space' (CW 19; 118).

Though O'Connor never wanted to overstep the boundaries of the artist in deep respect for Mystery, her constant attempt to create precision and in it depth or a 'consubstantiality of all things under God'[78] was motivated by her wish to disclose in her characters 'the mystery that [she] saw residing in the concrete'[79] for the benefit of her readers. She believed that 'man has fallen and that he is only perfectible by God's grace, not by his own unaided efforts. The Liberal approach is that man has never fallen, never incurred guilt, and is ultimately perfectible by his own efforts' (HB 302). But she was also aware of the fact that 'all human nature vigorously resists grace because grace changes us and the change is painful' (CW 1084). She wrote to 'A': 'Part of the difficulty of all this is that you write for an audience who doesn't know what

---

76 As an Aarhus University scholar, where we have a Steno Museum, I feel obliged to mention that O'Connor here is in unison with Niels Stensen's insight: 'Pulchra sunt quæ videntur, pulchriora quæ sciuntur, longe pulcherrima, quæ ignorantur'. *Opera philosophica* II, 254.

77 *On the Sublime*, chapter 7, quoted in Selden, op.cit. 153.

78 Trowbridge, Clinton W., 'The Comic Sense of Flannery O'Connor: Literalist of the Imagination'. *The Flannery O'Connor Bulletin*, vol. 12 (1983) 82.

79 Baker, J. Robert, 'Flannery O'Connor's Four-Fold Method of Allegory'. *The Flannery O'Connor Bulletin*, vol. 22 (1992) 85.

grace is and don't recognize it when they see it. All my stories are about the action of grace on a character who is not very willing to support it, but most people think of these stories as hard, hopeless, brutal, etc.' (CW 1067). But the characters are prepared for the moment of grace, O'Connor says, 'by the intensity of the evil circumstances' (CW 1119). As Bruce Bawer sums up O'Connor's treatment of her characters: 'O'Connor's barbs can sting. Yet her point is manifestly not to hold these characters up to ridicule, but rather to offer each of them as an example of a flawed and troubled human soul on its way to an epiphany'[80] or 'an awakening to all of reality as grace.'[81]

The triplex metaphoricity discussed above was, I think, seen by O'Connor as one. In the following I shall offer a brief sketch of O'Connor's work and of its critical reception, place her among other writers of the South and describe my own method of reading/reaching O'Connor through establishing the correct textual basis for the interpretation of a selection of her stories.

MYSTERY *THROUGH* MANNERS

Robert and Sally Fitzgerald's choice of *Mystery and Manners* as the title of their collection of Flannery O'Connor's occasional prose, a formulation they chose on the basis of one of O'Connor's posthumously published prose fragments (cp. MM 153), has influenced my work with O'Connor's oeuvre. The doubleness[82] indicated in this pair of concepts can also be found in the critical discussion of Flannery O'Connor's work. A substantial group of critics focusing on the content of O'Connor's works tend to classify her as a philosophical-religious mystic and

---

80 Op.cit. 317.
81 Kilcourse, op.cit. 37.
82 Frederick Asals has dealt with O'Connor's double vision in op.cit. 65-123. For an earlier discussion of this topic see my article 'Precision and Depth in Flannery O'Connor's Short Stories', *Rationality and the Liberal Spirit*, Centenary College of Louisiana, Shreveport, 1997, 149-61.
83 John R. May ('The Methodological Limits of Flannery O'Connor Critics', *The Flannery O'Connor Bulletin*, vol. 15, 1986, 16-28) thinks that every O'Connor critic must 'focus exclusively on the dimension of her religious world view and the manner in which it is achieved' (26). Similarly Harold Fickett says ('Why Do The Heathen Rage?' in *The Catholic World Report*, April 1992, 56-59) that 'O'Connor belongs to the company of the faithful. It won't do to join hands and celebrate her as an artist' (59).

prophet,[83] who through her strong images and her grotesque characters conjures up fallen mankind's basic situation, which can only be changed through the Creator's often shocking intervention with a new offer of salvation. In this group there are some who criticize O'Connor for the unorthodox way in which she deals with Christian revelation[84] or who distance themselves from her simply because of her Christian conviction.[85] Another steadily growing group of critics focus their interest on O'Connor's art and consider her well-founded in a narrative tradition which describes in minute details and very much to the point a way of life typical of the American South. They tend to ignore the content of her works and prefer to see O'Connor as a literary genius and a conscientiously working artist whose high artistic achievement cannot be contested.[86] Finally there is a group who work with both aspects in O'Connor's artistic universe. Titles like 'The Countryside and the True Country' (1962) for Robert Fitzgerald's early analysis of 'The Displaced Person', *The Added Dimension: The Art and Mind of Flannery O'Connor* (1977) for Melvin Friedman and L. Lawson's collection of es-

---

84   Ralph C. Wood classifies O'Connor as 'heterodox' ('The Heterodoxy of Flannery O'Connor's Book Reviews', *The Flannery O'Connor Bulletin*, vol. 5, 1976, 3-29) and André Bleikasten ('The Heresy of Flannery O'Connor' in Melvin J. Friedman and B.L. Clark, eds, *Critical Essays on Flannery O'Connor*, Boston, G.K. Hall, 1985, 138-158) concludes: 'The truth of O'Connor's work is the truth of her art, not that of her church. ... Pitting the supernatural against the natural in fierce antagonism, her theology holds nothing but scorn for everything human, and it is significant that in her work satanic evildoers (the 'Misfit', Rufus Johnson) are far less harshly dealt with than humanistic do-gooders (Rayber, Sheppard)' (156).

85   David Havird concludes in his secularized-sexualizing interpretation of four of O'Connor's short stories called 'The Saving Rape: Flannery O'Connor and Patriarchal Religion' (*The Mississippi Quarterly*, vol. 47, Winter 1993/94, no. 1, 15-26) among other things about Asbury Fox in 'The Enduring Chill': 'At the end of this story a male character lies sprawled on his bed, "[t]he old life in him ... exhausted," as a phallic Holy Ghost (represented by a birdlike water stain on the ceiling, a "fierce bird with [an] icicle in its beak" [374] descends upon him' (16).

86   Already in the special commemorative O'Connor issue of *Esprit* (vol. 8, Winter 1964) many contributors praised her art. Eudora Welty says here: 'She wrote with deep commitment about what put the greatest demands on her, and achieved a fiction of originality and power. ... I shall always treasure for my particular love and admiration her comic gifts. Work as good as hers makes all writers proud' (49). Harold Bloom ends his introduction to *Flannery O'Connor*, (New York, Chelsea House Publishers, 1986) as follows: 'Her pious admirers to the contrary, O'Connor would have bequeathed us even stronger novels and stories, of the eminence of Faulkner's, if she had been able to restrain her spiritual tendentiousness' (8).

says, Edward Kessler's *Flannery O'Connor's Language of Apocalypse* (1986) and Robert H. Brinkmeyer's *The Art & Vision of Flannery O'Connor* (1989) show the authors' interest in the surface and depth dimensions of O'Connor's works. In this context I should like to mention the doubleness in the title of the essay collection which Jan Nordby Gretlund and I edited in 1987. We chose to describe O'Connor as a *Realist of Distances*, the way in which she herself had characterized a prophet in her prose essay 'The Grotesque in Southern Fiction' (MM 44, 179).

My own interest in a close examination of the relation between 'mystery' and 'manners' in O'Connor's work was initiated by O'Connor's own description of the relationship between these two concepts. She formulates it as follows: 'The fiction writer presents mystery *through* manners, grace *through* nature [my emphases], but when he finishes there always has to be left over that sense of Mystery which cannot be accounted for by any human formula' (MM 153). 'Mystery' or the depth dimension, as I prefer to call it, is not thematized as such, O'Connor tries to show it *through* 'manners' or *through* precision in the description of detail. She had learned from the French scholastic Jacques Maritain that as an artist she had to manifest 'the invisible things by the visible'.[87] O'Connor wrote that 'art requires a delicate adjustment of the outer and inner worlds in such a way that, without changing their nature, they can be seen through each other' (MM 34-35). She sees it as her obligation to make her art perfect; then she has fulfilled her 'mission' as an artist and accomplished the story as an artwork. 'The artist has his hands full and does his duty if he attends to his art. ... art transcends its limitations only by staying within them' (MM 171), she says in her characteristically paradoxical way. The same she acknowledges among other things in Kipling's elegant way of describing the situation of the poor, while '[t]he mystery of existence is always shining through the texture of their ordinary lives' (MM 133). On the basis of O'Connor's own formulations I want to distance her from those critics who tend to declare her a Christian missionary, and from the ones who ignore or reject the depth dimension in her works. I intend to show that a paratactical treatment of 'mystery' and 'manners' does not correspond to the way in which O'Connor herself looked upon the two concepts and the way in which they are present in her works.

My method of entering into her work is to study the genesis of some

---

87 This sentence from *Art and Scholasticism* is quoted in Bieber, Christina, Op.cit. 44.

of her stories and on the basis of that to follow the artistic development of her entire work. Since her manuscripts are not available in facsimile and almost all manuscripts are collected in the Ina Dillard Russell Library in O'Connor's hometown of Milledgeville, Georgia, USA, which does not allow photocopying of the material, repeated research visits to the archive were necessary, which restricted the number of manuscripts I was able to work on. To have the opportunity to watch O'Connor, the artist, at work by collating the manuscripts, was a scholarly and intriguing experience, and I was soon convinced of O'Connor's determination to choose every single word and its placement precisely to fit the overall design of each story. The results of my research were published in *The Flannery O'Connor Bulletin* and elsewhere and they constitute part of the body of the present study.

FLANNERY O'CONNOR: RESPECTED WRITER OF THE SOUTH

Though O'Connor's oeuvre only comprises two collections of short stories – *A Good Man Is Hard To Find* (New York, 1955) and *Everything That Rises Must Converge* (New York, 1965) –, two novels – *Wise Blood* (New York, 1952) and *The Violent Bear It Away* (New York, 1960) –, a collection of talks and articles – *Mystery and Manners* (New York, 1969), – a substantial collection of letters – *The Habit of Being* (New York, 1979), – a collection of reviews – *The Presence of Grace* (The University of Georgia Press, 1983) – and a collection of interviews – *Conversations With Flannery O'Connor* (University Press of Mississippi, 1987) – one soon finds out that her works demand time and extended critical scrutiny. While criticism of her first works was mostly negative, O'Connor received in the last decade of her life considerable attention and positive recognition by other writers and critics. Three times she won The O. Henry Memorial Award, she received two State grants and a substantial Ford Foundation scholarship. Her works have been published again and again, last but not least in 1988 as *Flannery O'Connor: Collected Works* in The Library of America series, and her works have been translated into many languages. In Denmark her work has so far found limited response. In 1965 Grafisk Forlag published her first collection of short stories under the title *En god mand er svær at finde*. In recognition of the fact that she was little known in Denmark and only one of her works was available in Danish I tried in the early eighties to have her

second collection of short stories and a selection of her letters published in Danish. In 1984 I succeeded in having the second collection
of short stories translated and published by Katolsk Forlag under the
title *Skæringspunkt og andre noveller*.[88] In my introduction to this edition
I draw attention, among other things, to the fact that even if O'Connor's 'stories [are] entertaining, [they are] nevertheless always deeply
serious'. Much to my and other O'Connor scholars' surprise John
Huston's 1979 film version of O'Connor's characteristically Southern
and deeply religious first novel *Wise Blood*[89] was reviewed positively in
Denmark. As to Danish O'Connor criticism there is, apart from Jan
Nordby Gretlund's work, only Erik Nielsen's perceptive analysis of her
novels in his monograph *Flannery O'Connors Romaner* (Odense, Odense
Universitetsforlag, 1992). My review of Erik Nielsen's monograph emphasizes his cogent analyses and the way in which he sees her work in
a Nordic perspective, particularly taking into consideration the Danish
reader, who is not familiar with O'Connor's universe. A quotation from
Erik Nielsen's precise characterization of O'Connor's poetics, which
takes the concrete as the starting point of all poetry, is worth repeating
here: Erik Nielsen has a clear perception of 'how narrowly and consciously Flannery O'Connor's art is connected with her production
ethics, reception theory, practice of taste, religion, moral views, philosophy, ethics, and her entire way of experiencing the world. O'Connor's
understanding of existence seems to be entirely without contradic-
tions.[90] All the many areas are joined together organically by a homo-
geneous view of life'.[91]

The number of critics aware of Flannery O'Connor's work can be

---

88 The Danish writer Bo Green Jensen ends his fine review of this publication with the
   recommendation: 'Hvis man læser én amerikansk bog i år, så lad det blive denne'. (If
   you only read one American book this year, let it be this one. *Afstandens indsigt*,
   København, Borgen, 1985, 119.) Because of shortage of space the story 'A View of
   the Woods' was not included in this edition.
89 This was John Huston's last film. Recently Michael Kreyling has presented new *Wise
   Blood* criticism and collected four new approaches to the novel in *New Essays on*
   Wise Blood, (Boston, Cambridge University Press, 1995).
90 This unified picture of reality has first been dealt with extensively in John F.
   Desmond's *Risen Sons: Flannery* O'Connor's *Vision of History* (Athens, University of
   Georgia Press, 1987). He says among other things: 'Flannery O'Connor's fiction is all
   of a piece. Probably more than any American writer of her generation, she managed
   to create a coherent wholeness of vision and form' (12).
91 Erik Nielsen, *Flannery O'Connors Romaner*, 295.

seen in the fact that there are more than fifty monographs and more than three hundred scholarly articles about her.[92] Even though some critics look negatively upon O'Connor's *Weltanschauung*, they nevertheless recognize her artistic ability. As early as 1952 the English novelist Evelyn Waugh said about O'Connor's first novel *Wise Blood*: 'If this is really the unaided work of a young lady, it is a remarkable product'.[93]

O'Connor's reputation is also attested by the many letters from and interviews with contemporary authors such as Katherine Anne Porter, Eudora Welty, Walker Percy, John Hawkes and Robert Drake. A number of late 20th-century authors such as Joyce Carol Oates, Paula Sharp,[94] Rudy Wiebe, Sheldon Currie, Jack Hodgins, Alice Munro, Joan MacLeod,[95] Raymond Carver, Bobbie Ann Mason, Alistair MacLeod readily acknowledge, that Flannery O'Connor's works were of great importance for their own way of writing: The Canadian author Alistair MacLeod said to me on November 10, 1990: 'A modern short story writer can hardly avoid being influenced by her'. 'I can't imagine writing anything, ever, if I had not read Flannery O'Connor', said Southern author Lee Smith on 'The Habit of Art' conference in Milledgeville, 1994. The English novelist Marina Warner told me during a writers' seminar in Århus on April 30, 1996, that O'Connor's 'writing is fantastic' and she mentioned especially the short story 'The Artificial Nigger' as a work of genius.[96] The Australian novelist and short story

---

92 According to R. Neil Scott's account (*The Flannery O'Connor Bulletin*, vol. 19, 1990, 77-99) on University Microfilm International's database there were already in 1990 no less than 170 Ph.D. theses on Flannery O'Connor.

93 Quoted by Sally Fitzgerald, HB 35.

94 At 'The Habit of Art' Conference on O'Connor in Milledgeville, 1994, Marshall Bruce Gentry drew attention to O'Connor's legacy in Joyce Carol Oates' story 'Where Are You Going, Where Have You Been?' and in Paula Sharp's story 'A Meeting on the Highway'. See also Gentry's article in *The Flannery O'Connor Bulletin* vol. 23, 1994-95, 44-60, where he cites H. Bloom for having called O'Connor 'Oates's inescapable precursor' (44).

95 In 'Some Glimpses of Flannery O'Connor in the Canadian Landscape' (*The Flannery O'Connor Bulletin*, vol. 23, 1994-95, 83-90) Frederick Asals quotes Alice Munro for having claimed 'When I was starting I wrote ... imitation Flannery O'Connor stories' (84) and playwright Joan MacLeod's admiration for O'Connor seems unrestricted: 'All rumors are true – I adore Flannery O'Connor. ... without question she is the writer that influenced me most' (87-88). Asals also mentions O'Connor's influence on Jack Hodgins, Isabel Huggan and Deborah Joy Corey.

96 This short story was also O'Connor's own favorite, when she was asked to read from her work. 'I suppose "The Artificial Nigger" is my favorite' (HB 101), she wrote on September 6, 1955 to her friend 'A'.

writer Beverley Farmer in a letter to me of May 2, 1996 summarized Flannery O'Connor's influence in Australia: 'Her image is rather like that of a prose Emily Dickinson – fierce, original, elliptical, an eccentric recluse and visionary, a pioneer. Many of the big names in the fiction of the last two decades, in Australia as elsewhere, have sat at her feet at some point in their writing lives. … Her influence is clearest in the work of Tim Winton'. The fact that Loren Logsdon and Charles W. Mayer in 1987 called their collection of essays on the present situation of the American short story *Since Flannery O'Connor* indicates that her work is regarded as a milestone in the history of short-story writing in the 20th century.[97] Sally Fitzgerald, O'Connor's close friend, editor and biographer, concludes against the background of the extensive critical literature on O'Connor: 'Evidently she cannot be dismissed in silence'.[98] Ashley Brown places O'Connor among the greatest in the American tradition of fiction: 'Flannery O'Connor's stories take their place in the great American tradition of short fiction, and one can already see her as the heir to Hawthorne, Poe, Stephen Crane, and a dozen of others'.[99]

As we have seen, O'Connor took her vocation as an artist very seriously and she was always aware of her Southernness, which she regarded as 'a gateway to reality' (MM 54). One of her highest artistic goals was to render even the smallest detail of experience in very concrete images, which at the same time let the unknown shine through as in a revelation. 'The longer you look at one object, the more of the world you see in it' (MM 77). In order to find the structure that fitted her stories best and in order to find the expression that covered her vision most appropriately, O'Connor meticulously revised her texts again and again, and she practiced this discipline also in the last days before her death.

Flannery O'Connor left a rich collection of manuscripts, which thanks to her mother's gift in 1970 are collected in the Ina Dillard Russell Library, Georgia College, Milledgeville, Georgia, USA. This collection is unique, because it does not only contain almost all surviving

---

97 Waldemar Zacharasiewics has discussed O'Connor from the angle of reception history and looked at her influence on later short-story writers especially in Canada. In 'From the State to the Strait of Georgia: Aspects of the Response by Some of Flannery O'Connor's Creative Readers' (in *Realist of Distances*, Karl-Heinz Westarp & Jan N. Gretlund, eds [Århus, Aarhus University Press, 1987], 171-184) Zacharasiewics argues that the narrator in Rudy Wiebe's short story 'Did Jesus Ever Laugh?' (1970) is a character clearly influenced by O'Connor's cold-blooded killer 'The Misfit'.
98 'Degrees and Kinds' in *Realist of Distances*, 16.
99 'Flannery O'Connor: A Literary Memoir' in *Realist of Distances*, 29.

manuscripts of O'Connor's short stories, novels and prose writings, but also the main part of her library, comments on the contents of which are available in an edition by Arthur F. Kinney under the title *Flannery O'Connor's Library: Resources of Being*. Since the O'Connor collection was opened to scholars in 1972, the manuscripts were first systematized by Robert Dunn. In 1989 Stephen G. Driggers edited the collection in revised form under the title *The Manuscripts of Flannery O'Connor at Georgia College*. In Driggers the manuscripts are contained in 905 folders and 297 files.

ESTABLISHING THE CORRECT TEXT: MANUSCRIPT STUDIES

I started my manuscript studies during a research trip to the US in 1982 and thus before the edition by Driggers. It was very difficult to form an overview of the collection, because the systematization was not finished and because the library's very strict manuscript rules did not allow photocopying of the material. All manuscript details had to be registered and copied by hand – with the resulting risk of mistakes. I continued my research during a period at the Ina Dillard Russell Library in 1988 and a visit in 1994. The many manuscript versions of the single texts, the numerous deletions, changes and additions show even at a first glance unmistakably that O'Connor was a painstakingly and diligently working writer. She corrected her texts from the first draft till the final typed version. Corrections and changes are hand-written – in pencil or ink – or typed, and they comprise major changes of structure as well as changes of language down to single words or syllables. She was self-critical enough not to rely on her own artistic judgment alone, she sent her texts to a number of friends, some of whom were authors themselves, and asked them for comments. These she incorporated or rejected depending on what her artistic sense commanded. A good case in point is O'Connor's critical response to changes in the penultimate version of 'Judgement Day' suggested by her friend Catherine Carver. In my article '"Judgement Day": The Published Text *versus* Flannery O'Connor's Final Version' and in Chapter II I have given a detailed analysis of these changes.

O'Connor's letters, collected and edited by Sally Fitzgerald in *The Habit of Being*, also prove her constant fight for *le mot juste*. One of many examples is found in a letter of November 23, 1963 where O'Connor asked her friend 'A' for help in connection with a draft of 'Revelation': 'I have no idea if it works or not, particularly the last paragraph. I started to let it end where the hogs pant with a secret life, but I thought something else was needed. Maybe not what I've got. But anyway, anything you have to say will be helpful' (HB 549). Precision was the most important artistic goal for Flannery O'Connor, but she was also aware of the depth, which she wanted her stories to contain and which could only become visible in and through the precision of detail: the choice of characters, of situations, of images, of language levels, of single words and sounds must be seen as a function of O'Connor's attempt to describe the human situation as concretely and realistically as possible. In the description of mankind's immanent situation the transcendent dimension should shine up, become translucent as in an epiphany. This combination of depth *through* detail is, as I have mentioned above, the trademark of Flannery O'Connor's art. In my manuscript studies and in my analyses I have therefore worked with the double aim of establishing the correct manuscript basis and relating this to the interpretation of the texts' depth.

My interest in the manuscripts was sharpened, when I became aware of the fact that O'Connor throughout her career had worked with and revised one particular narrative material. It is her first short story 'The Geranium', which was published in *Accent* (6, Summer, 1946), 245-53. She used this text also as part of her MFA-thesis, which she handed in for adjudication at Iowa State University in June 1947. The letters show that she worked on the same material again at the end of 1954 now entitled 'An Exile in the East'. She was, however, not satisfied with the result and therefore this version was not included in her first collection of stories *A Good Man Is Hard to Find*. 'An Exile in the East' was first published in 1978 by Jan Nordby Gretlund in *The South Carolina Review* vol. 11, (November, 1978), 12-21. But O'Connor did not discard the story (HB 88). By the end of 1963 she was working on a new version under the title 'Getting Home'. This version was first published in 1993 in my synoptic variorum edition of these manuscripts under the title *Flannery O'Connor: The Growing Craft*. In a late manuscript (Dunn 194d, Driggers 208d) she replaced the title 'Getting Home' with 'Judgement Day', the title under which the story was published in O'Connor's second collection *Everything That Rises Must Converge*. O'Connor worked on this story and 'Parker's Back' during the very last days before her death on August 3, 1964. Robert Giroux posthumously arranged the edition of *Everything That Rises Must Converge* and he honored the list of contents, on which O'Connor had agreed with him and her literary agent Eliza-beth McKee during the spring of 1964. O'Connor's development from 'The Geranium' to 'Judgement Day' was first dealt with by Ralph C. Wood in *The Flannery O'Connor Bulletin* vol. 7, 1978 under the title 'From Fashionable Tolerance to Unfashionable Redemption' and 'the spiritual and aesthetic distance traversed' by O'Connor in this period was characterized by Harold Bloom as 'a matter not of decades but of light years'.[100]

'"Judgement Day": The Published Text *versus* Flannery O'Connor's Final Version' presents the result of manuscript comparisons and par-allel analyses of O'Connor's letters from the spring of 1964. The com-parison showed that there were discrepancies between the published version of 'Judgement Day' and one of the manuscripts with O'Con-nor's handwritten corrections. I found that the published version of 'Judgment [*sic*] Day' is based on a manuscript of 15 pages (Dunn 197a, Driggers 211a), a carbon copy of which O'Connor on June 27, 1964 had sent to her friend Catherine Carver with the request to look at it with a view to possible changes and its suitability for *Everything That Rises Must Converge*. This carbon copy is also kept in the manuscript collec-tion (Dunn 197b, Driggers 211b). In it there are comments, questions and suggestions for changes in a hand which used a blue color pen. By comparisons of handwriting in other documents in the collection I detected that this was Catherine Carver's hand. The same carbon copy also shows changes in O'Connor's almost illegible late hand. That means that Carver had returned the copy very quickly, because O'Connor comments upon and rejects some of Carver's suggestions in a letter to her of July 15, 1964. In all Carver had used her pen twenty-nine times in the text itself and thirty-nine times in the margin. O'Con-nor incorporated most of the suggestions, thus giving the short story a form that better satisfied her aesthetic sense, what I hope to have shown in '"Judgement Day": The Published Text *versus* Flannery O'Connor's Final Version' through my detailed analysis of the individ-ual changes. However, those last changes were left out in the published version of 'Judgement Day', because Robert Giroux apparently was not aware of the existence of this carbon copy of the story when he pre-pared the second collection for publication. After the publication of my findings in 1982 in *The Flannery O'Connor Bulletin*, most of O'Connor's

---

100 Op.cit. VII.

latest changes were adopted into the standard edition of her works *Flannery O'Connor: Collected Works*,[101] which was edited by Sally Fitzgerald, while Driggers – without due reference – uses my results but does not seem to be aware of the fact that the changes actually were included in O'Connor's collected works.[102] My research on the 'Judgement-Day' material was continued in 'Flannery O'Connor's Development: An Analysis of the Judgement-Day Material' and brought to completion in *Flannery O'Connor: The Growing Craft*, which tries to prove the unique status of the 'Judgement-Day' material in O'Connor's work. During my research visit to the Ina Dillard Russell Library in 1988 it was my goal to copy all manuscripts and manuscript fragments related to the different forms that this material had in the course of O'Connor's career. In his edition of 'An Exile in the East' Jan Nordby Gretlund had already in 1978 drawn attention to the stylistic and structural development 'The Geranium' had undergone, after O'Connor had rewritten it in 1954. In a first attempt I tried, in 'Flannery O'Connor's Development: An Analysis of the Judgement-Day Material', to relate the development, which this narrative material had undergone from 'The Geranium' (1946), through 'An Exile in the East' and 'Getting Home' (1963-64) to the final version in 'Judgement Day' (1964), to Flannery O'Connor's own development as artist and thinker. In this article I have given a short characterization of the successive versions of the story, which not only shows the growing complexity in the structure and in the imagery but also on the basis of this the new depth dimensions it reaches. From a simple story about an old white man from the South, who in the cold atmosphere of New York is longing back to the more human milieu of the South, it grows into a highly dramatic narrative about man's pilgrimage towards death and judgment.

---

101 CW, 1259-1260: 'The importance of the carbon typescript was recognized and is described by Karl-Heinz Westarp in *The Flannery O'Connor Bulletin*, vol. 11, 1982, pp. 108-22'.

102 Driggers, (130) says in connection with 211a: 'One significant correction in the published version occurs on p. 4 of this MS, where Tanner says, "You promised you'd bury me here." The published story correctly substitutes "there" for "here"'. In note 7 of my article on 'Judgement Day', I commented on this passage in the story: 'With no authority in Dunn 194a, ... p. 4, the posthumous editors replaced – quite in keeping with the context – "there" for the manuscript's "here"'. Driggers accepts my proof, however, since he mentions Catherine Carver as the source of the MS-comments in blue color pen.

During my work with 'Flannery O'Connor's Development: An Analysis of the Judgement-Day Material' I came to realize the necessity of presenting my thesis in a more detailed manner. I therefore started a comparative arrangement of all manuscripts related to the 'Judgement-Day' material. My goal was not only to publish the manuscripts and thus make them more easily accessible to scholars who do not have the privilege of traveling to the O'Connor Collection in Milledgeville, but also to visualize Flannery O'Connor's work with the manuscripts by placing the four basic versions side by side. This idea was inspired by the new computer-based synoptic edition of James Joyce's *Ulysses*, which Hans Walter Gabler and his team after seven years of compilatory work had published with Garland (New York) in 1984. By means of a very complicated apparatus of notes Gabler had been able to show the development of the text on the left page of this edition and the resulting 'final' text on the right page. I changed Gabler's way of presenting the variants, because I wanted to show all the text-variants *in* the text and in their right context; through this I hoped to be able to avoid the usual critical apparatus at the bottom of the page. After four years of preparatory work for the publication of *Flannery O'Connor: The Growing Craft* the solution I adopted in the end was to render each manuscript in separate typeface. In this way the reader can follow the development of each single manuscript and of the manuscripts in relation to each other. Apart from that the four basic versions of the story are placed in columns side by side. Through this synoptic arrangement of the twenty-seven manuscripts and my addition of the relevant page- and line-numbers of the cross-references it becomes possible to see how O'Connor moved single elements from one place in the story to another, which parts she added or deleted in the different stages of the development and how the story's size and the precision of its language grew. A first glance at the synoptically arranged material surprises because of the many 'empty' columns; these 'lacunae', however, show how the material grew from the first to the last version. It is also noticeable that there is not a word-to-word synopsis in all cases, but an attempt to do that would have rendered the text less clear. I hope that this comparative reading is manageable for the reader with the present shape of *The Growing Craft* in hand.[103]

---

103 In his review of the book Marshall Bruce Gentry wrote: 'Anyone who wants to analyze any of these related stories in the future will need to examine this book' (*The Flannery O'Connor Bulletin*, vol. 22, 1993/94, 138).

It was in *Flannery O'Connor: The Growing Craft* that these manu-scripts were published and thus the third version of the story, 'Getting Home', was made available in print for the first time. The aim with this new form of manuscript editing is to make the texts more easily ap-proachable, to give the reader – and especially young authors – the op-portunity to see a writer at work, to learn from O'Connor's process of composition, and finally to be able to follow her artistic development from first to last. In my introduction to *The Growing Craft* I have given an appraisal of Flannery O'Connor's importance, especially in relation to the short-story tradition of the South. Apart from that I have ac-counted for the position of these manuscripts in her career, I have char-acterized the individual manuscripts and in this connection drawn at-tention to some malplacements in Driggers. I have also given a survey of the way in which the manuscript material has been arranged. Al-ready in '"Judgement Day": The Published Text *versus* Flannery O'Con-nor's Final Version' I had exemplified O'Connor's search for the 'right' word, and on pages XXV-XXIX of *The Growing Craft* I have described her technique, among other things by a detailed analysis of the open-ing paragraphs of the short story.

LOOKING FOR THE DEPTH DIMENSION

With *The Growing Craft* I finished this part of my research project, the aim of which was to show Flannery O'Connor's growing artistic preci-sion and in consequence thereof the greater intensity and depth of vi-sion in the 'Judgement-Day' material. During my work with 'Judgement Day' I became aware of the technical brilliance and the theological themes of Flannery O'Connor's very last short story 'Parker's Back'. I tried to solve some of the riddles of this story in '"Parker's Back": A Curious Crux Concerning Its Sources' and in 'Teilhard de Chardin's Im-pact on Flannery O'Connor: A Reading of "Parker's Back"', on which Chapter IV of the present study is based. O'Connor mentions this story for the first time in a letter of December 24, 1960 to her friend 'A', but according to a letter of January 27, 1961 she put it aside, because she was dissatisfied with its present tone which she considered 'too funny to be serious as it ought' (HB 427). Instead she concentrated work on a story, which she eventually gave the Teilhard de Chardin inspired title 'Everything That Rises Must Converge' (Tout ce qui monte converge). As late as June 9, 1964 she planned to continue work on 'Parker's Back'.

In spite of the little energy left in the last days of her life she sent a copy of 'Parker's Back' to 'A' on the 11th of July. 'A' very quickly commented on the text, for already on July 17 O'Connor sent her 'a better barroom scene' (HB 593). Caroline Gordon Tate also gave her good pieces of advice about possible changes. When her friend 'A' apparently misunderstood the meaning of the tattooed protagonist completely, O'Connor wrote again to her on July 25 – that is nine days before her death – and suggested a key to an interpretation.

In 'Parker's Back' O'Connor shows detailed knowledge of tattooing and in her letter to 'A' of July 17 she refers to a book edited by Peter Leighton, *Memoirs of a Tattooist* (London, 1958), as the source of her knowledge. The book is based on letters, notes and diary entries by George Burchett, who was known as 'King of Tattooists'.[104] Through a comparative analysis of O'Connor's story and *Memoirs* I was able to show in '"Parker's Back": A Curious Crux Concerning Its Sources', that Flannery O'Connor had taken a number of details from *Memoirs*. But there was an essential element in the story that still needed further explanation, I thought: what was the source of the centrally placed image of the Byzantine Christ. I did not consider a small copy of this picture in one of the books in O'Connor's library a sufficient explanation, nor did I think that the postcard featuring the Pantocrator from Daphni Monastery near Athens, that W. A. Sessions and his wife Jenny sent to O'Connor from Greece in 1961,[105] could be sufficient sources for the figure of the Byzantine Christ in 'Parker's Back'. In my search for other possible explanations Gerald Becham, former curator of the O'Connor Collection in the Ina Dillard Russell Library, drew my attention to an article from 1973 in the *Atlanta Journal and Constitution Magazine* about a second generation Georgian tattoo artist called Ted Don Inman, who among his tattooing motives mentioned pictures of Christ, among those a Byzantine head of Christ. Among other details in the article, which could suggest that O'Connor had known Inman's father's tattooing work, was the following information: 'And then once, I put the head of Christ on a buddy's back. I guess that's my best tattoo'. The fact that such a newspaper article could have spurred O'Connor's vision seems

---

104 He remembers among other things the occasion when the Danish King Frederik IXth was tattooed by him in London.

105 The information and a black-and-white copy of the picture are given in *Flannery O'Connor and the Christian Mystery*, ed. by John J. Murphy, Brigham Young University, Salt Lake City, Utah, 1997, 193.

all the more plausible, since she is known to have used local newspapers as sources of inspiration also in other instances. I succeeded in locating Ted Inman Jr., who in an interview told me that his father probably in 1960 had had an interview with reprints of some of his tattoos in the local paper in Augusta, Georgia, *The Augusta Chronicle*, but that he himself unfortunately did not have a copy of the article. My microfilm viewing in the Augusta Public Library of the paper's entire year 1960 did not lead to a solution of the riddle. I was therefore very glad to see that James F. Farnham, who after having corresponded with Flannery O'Connor around Easter 1963 had visited her in Milledgeville, in the 1983 volume of *The Flannery O'Connor Bulletin* took up my idea and presented further evidence for my theory about the source of the Byzantine Christ in 'Parker's Back'. He thinks that O'Connor must have seen the newspaper article in the spring of 1963, for in the course of their conversation she had said that she had just read a newspaper article about a man who had had a Christ tattooed on his back. She said: 'I wonder what it's like when you have to go out and get Jesus tattooed on your back!'[106] The article itself has not yet been found, and the distance has so far made it impossible for me to investigate the question further, but as Farnham says: 'Perhaps the detective work so well begun by Westarp will be concluded, and we then may have a more complete understanding of the imaginative gestation of one of O'Connor's most distinguished stories'.[107]

The imagery in 'Parker's Back' with Parker, who is tattooed all over, at the center, is so surprising and strong that it reminds one of John Donne's 'metaphysical' images.[108] I think that critical explanations of the images as grotesque are not satisfactory, because O'Connor especially in her last stories very consciously chose her images to underline the philosophic-theological depth dimension of the stories. Looking through O'Connor's library convinced me of her great interest in traditional and modern scholastic thinking represented in the works of

---

106 James S. Farnham, 'Further Evidence for the Sources of "Parker's Back"' in *The Flannery O'Connor Bulletin* vol. 12, 1983, 115.

107 Ibid. 116.

108 In his article 'What you Can't Talk About' in Harold Bloom, ed. *Flannery O'Connor*, (New York, Chelsea House Publishers, 1986, 127-34) John Burt adduces an incisive analysis of 'Parker's Back', the story which Harold Bloom calls 'a great, somber story' and a fine example of O'Connor's 'most authentic spiritual vision' (Ibid. VIII).

Thomas Aquinas and of Jacques Maritain.[109] The French paleontologist, philosopher and theologian Pierre Teilhard de Chardin's thinking was of special interest to O'Connor. She carefully studied and reviewed three of his major works – her marginal notes in the texts are proof of this – and the same is true of four monographs about him. How familiar she was with Chardin's way of thinking and how fascinated she was with it can among other things be seen in the fact that she chose a centrally placed Chardin adage as the title for her cover story of the second collection of short stories *Everything That Rises Must Converge*. According to her letters she started reading Teilhard at the end of 1959[110] and several letters to friends since then prove that she warmly recommended the reading of his works to acquaintances and friends.[111] She saw her own vocation as a writer closely related to Teilhard's prophetic thinking, which – according to O'Connor's review of de Chardin's book *The Phenomenon of Man* – was described by Julian Huxley in his introduction to Chardin's book as the triple synthesis 'of the material and physical world with mind and spirit; of the past with the future; and of variety with unity, the many with the one'.[112]

As mentioned above, O'Connor commenced work on the composition of 'Parker's Back' late in 1960, when under the influence of her reading of Teilhard de Chardin. In 'Teilhard de Chardin's Impact on Flannery O'Connor: A Reading of "Parker's Back"', I relate the precision in O'Connor's choice of interconnected images in 'Parker's Back' to the story's philosophic-theological depth. I try to make probable a reading of the story as a poetic rendering of Teilhard's evolutionary theory, which counts on the convergence of history towards the point Omega, which is Christ. In Parker's wife Sarah Ruth, Flannery O'Connor has in an ingenious way incorporated in the story a centrally placed critic of pictures in general but especially of the picture of Christ. Sarah Ruth, who upon the sight of Christ's picture tattooed on Parker's back shouts: 'Idolatry! Enflaming yourself with idols under every green tree!

---

109 In his essay on the story 'Revelation' Sura P. Rath talks about a 'Thomistic Resolution' and says that O'Connor's 'acknowledgement of her debt to St. Thomas appears ubiquitously in her writings, both in private letters to friends and in published book reviews and public lectures' (*The Flannery O'Connor Bulletin*, vol. 19, 1990, 1).

110 HB 366, 368.

111 C. Ralph Stephens, ed., *The Correspondence of Flannery O'Connor and the Brainard Cheneys*, University Press of Mississippi, 1986, 160.

112 Reprinted in Lorine M. Getz, op.cit. 56.

I can put up with lies and vanity but I don't want an idolater in this house!' (CW 674) I argue that Sarah Ruth wants to cultivate spiritual values only and despise God's epiphany or incarnation in the physical world of the senses. She says about God: 'He don't look. ... He's a spirit' (CW 674).[113] She does not connect, as Teilhard de Chardin did, the physical with the spiritual reality. But Parker does this: in the end his body becomes transparent.[114] I think the pictures are put onto his body in a succession similar to the way in which the universe evolved according to Teilhard de Chardin with a convergence toward *homo sapiens*. At the end the Spirit – the Word – is made flesh in the Incarnation, and by having the picture of Christ tattooed on his back Parker becomes an *alter Christus*, who like Jesus Christ is rejected by mankind, in the story represented by his wife Sarah Ruth.

In this unique way Flannery O'Connor in 'Parker's Back' has dramatized de Chardin's scientific-philosophic-theological vision of the history of the universe from the beginning to its completion in the cosmic point Omega. As mentioned earlier, O'Connor was deeply concerned about the 'tone' of the story, it should not be 'too funny', but even in its published version, 'Parker's Back' catches the reader by its persistently ironic tone. Both O.E. Parker and his wife Sarah Ruth and their behavior as a married couple are ridiculed. One example must suffice: When Parker makes advances to her, she throws him out of her truck. 'He made up his mind then and there to have nothing further to do with her. They were married in the County Ordinary's office because Sarah Ruth thought churches were idolatrous. ... Marriage did not change Sarah Ruth a jot and it made Parker gloomier than ever' (CS 518). The reader is held in suspense by a meticulously planned narrative not dissimilar to the spider-web of tattoos on Parker's body. The wealth of carefully interwoven images keeps the reader questioning their meaning, which only starts revealing itself after repeated readings.

One of the dimensions which O'Connor critics were late in detect-

---

113 Dennis Patrick Slattery has from a different angle reached similar results in his essay 'Evil and the Negation of the Body: Flannery O'Connor's "Parker's Back"' (*The Flannery O'Connor Bulletin*, vol. 17, 1988, 69-79). Frederick Asals has in his essay '"Obediah," "Obadiah": *Guys and Dolls* and "Parker's Back"' (*The Flannery O'Connor Bulletin*, vol. 21, 1992, 37-42) over and above parallels in names detected a structural and thematic affinity between the two works mentioned.

114 Frederick Asals says in *The Imagination of Extremity*, 66, that O'Connor in her last works again and again insists 'that existence can only be *in* the body, *in* matter, whatever horrors that may entail' (Asals' emphases).

ing is her interest both privately and in her fiction in social issues,[115] often used as the starting-point of a story and as a means of giving a detailed depiction of Southern milieu. In 'Flannery O'Connor's Displaced Persons', which is an analysis of her short story from 1953-54 with the title 'The Displaced Person'[116] and in Chapter V below I have described O'Connor's use of a concrete social event in order to throw light upon one of the metaphysical convictions, which is centrally placed in her universe. The concrete occasion is the fate of a Polish immigrant family on a farm in the South. Leonard M. Olschner in his essay 'Annotations on History and Society in Flannery O'Connor's "The Displaced Person"' has accounted for the many 'DPs', who flooded the USA in the post-war years, and for their special circumstances in the South. He states that among the first 813 DPs, who arrived in New York on October 30, 1948, there were 388 Catholics from Poland.[117] In O'Connor's short story all social layers are represented on the farm: Mrs. McIntyre, the white owner, the Shortleys, a white family of farm workers, a couple of blacks, the Polish Mr. Guizac with his family[118] and the Catholic priest, who had brought the Polish family to their new environment. O'Connor depicts the social differences between characters by showing their different ways of behavior, which is partly due to their cultural background. Mr. Guizac, the title figure of the 'Displaced Person', is diligent and efficient, a reason for the other employees on the farm to regard him as a threat, while the owner increasingly regards him as a gain. When the Shortleys are about to be laid off, because Guizac's efficiency has rendered them superfluous, Mrs. Shortley dies of shock because of the impending humiliation. However, when Guizac plans a 'family-reunion' by trying to bring one of his family members over from Poland, the owner also turns against him. Prompted by a revengeful Mr. Shortley she fears that Guizac plans to take over the farm. Therefore she tacitly accepts that Shortley lets the wheel of a

---

115 Jan Nordby Gretlund describes O'Connor's 'middle period' as the one when as a social satirist she is most aware of social questions (cp. 'The Side of the Road: Flannery O'Connor's Social Sensibility' in *Realist of Distances*, 197-207).

116 This story does not exist in manuscript form. In the collection it is only represented in the final text of *A Good Man Is Hard To Find*.

117 *The Flannery O'Connor Bulletin*, vol. 16, 1987, 62-77.

118 In 1952 Flannery O'Connor's mother hired a Polish refugee family whose name was Matisiack. They were successful and still lived on the O'Connor farm, when Flannery was working on this story in 1954. (Cp. C. Ralph Stephens, ed., *The Correspondence of Flannery O'Connor and the Brainard Cheneys*, 17 n.)

tractor run over Guizac and kill him. In this way Guizac becomes – on a different level – a 'Displaced Person'.[119] O'Connor here describes the fate of an immigrant quite concretely, but underneath the story's humorous, interesting and shocking surface the reader senses a deeper form of 'displacement': O'Connor sees man as *homo viator*, always on the way and alienated in this life. But this dimension has been forgotten and the meeting with Guizac results in a conversion of the other main characters in the story: they learn to see themselves in their existential 'exile'. Thus Guizac's status as refugee has been given universal and metaphysical depth.[120]

Throwing light on the depth dimension in O'Connor's short story 'The Lame Shall Enter First' from 1962 is also one of the aims of my analyses in 'Shades of Evil in the Fictions of Flannery O'Connor and Walker Percy' and 'Conceptions of Mystery in Eudora Welty and Flannery O'Connor', on which Chapter VI of the present study is based. Another aim is to show parallels and contrasts between O'Connor and two other centrally placed Southern authors, i.e. Walker Percy[121] and Eudora Welty,[122] who both knew O'Connor and who, as can be seen in their letters were highly appreciative of her art. In 'Shades of Evil in the Fictions of Flannery O'Connor and Walker Percy' I start by accounting for Percy's and O'Connor's understanding of evil, and in 'Conceptions of Mystery in Eudora Welty and Flannery O'Connor' I

119 In his otherwise rather critical review of *Where? Place in Recent North American Fiction* (K.-H. Westarp, ed., Århus, Aarhus Universitetsforlag, 1991) James M. Mellard says, '[Westarp] interprets "The Displaced Person" correctly, but he fails to see that place is simply not the issue for O'Connor' (*The Mississippi Quarterly*, vol. 45, Spring 1992, no. 2, 200).

120 Olschner reached a similar conclusion: 'All of us are, in fact, DPs. Contemporary history thus becomes not a mere thematic quarry for fiction but rather an analogy, in O'Connor's eschatological argument, for humankind's condition on earth' (Op.cit. 75).

121 See my Preface to Jan Nordby Gretlund & K.-H. Westarp, eds, *Walker Percy: Novelist & Philosopher* (Jackson, University Press of Mississippi, 1991, IX-XIV), where I give a general characterization of Walker Percy's novels, and my essay 'Message to the Lost Self: Percy's Analysis of the Human Situation' (*Renascence*, vol. XLIV, no. 3, 1992, 216-24), where I discuss the presentation of the human situation in Percy's prose work *Lost in the Cosmos*, which focuses on the 'Fall' as much of O'Connor's work does.

122 In 'Beyond Loss: Eudora Welty's *Losing Battles*' (Jan Nordby Gretlund & K.-H. Westarp, eds, *The Late Novels of Eudora Welty*, Columbia, University of South Carolina Press, 1998, 56-66) I try to prove the presence of a 'beyond' also in Welty's fiction.

describe Welty's and O'Connor's understanding of 'mystery'.[123] I chose to deal with 'The Lame Shall Enter First', because we have in this story a detailed description of the battle between the seemingly 'good' Sheppard and the seemingly 'evil' Rufus Johnson, whom O'Connor called 'one of Tarwater's[124] terrible cousins' (HB 456). O'Connor understood evil as a living reality, which is seen concretely at work in several of her characters, and she sees a deep experiential connection between evil and life's deep dimensions: 'To insure our sense of mystery, we need a sense of evil' (MM 117), she said. The way to reach the depth dimension is to see and describe reality as concretely and in as detailed a manner as possible. In this way the word of fiction can strengthen the reader's understanding of the 'mystery' of reality. The interaction in fiction between the outer appearance, – 'manners' – and the deep meaning – 'mystery'– renders it an 'incarnational art',[125] because it deals 'with all those concrete details of life that make actual the mystery of our position on earth' (MM 68).

One of the technically most striking areas where precise descriptive detail is of particular importance for the rendering of depth of vision and meaning is Flannery O'Connor's depiction of settings. In 'Flannery O'Connor's Translucent Settings' and in Chapter III below I argue that her settings are 'translucent' – allowing light to pass through and be diffused –. Her settings are dramatically important factors in defining the characters in their relation to each other and on their way towards anagnorisis, their moment of grace. Her tree lines in particular are seen to be on the cutting edge between immanence and transcendence, where the character in an epiphanic moment of revelation may experience the true depth of existence and where O'Connor's art is most clearly incarnational.

---

123 Paul W. Nisly has treated the two concepts as one in 'The Mystery of Evil: Flannery O'Connor's Gothic Power' (*The Flannery O'Connor Bulletin*, vol. 11, 1982, 25-35).

124 Tarwater is the protagonist in *The Violent Bear It Away*.

125 John Desmond uses the concept 'incarnational art' for his approach to O'Connor in his monograph *Risen Sons*: 'The essential problem remained the same throughout [O'Connor's] career: how to create images that would "connect" the Incarnation with fictional incarnation, Mystery with mystery [O'Connor herself used the distinction between mystery and Mystery {MM 153}] – the "two points" of light which she attempted to incarnate within a single dramatic image' (32). Against Desmond's description of a duality in O'Connor's creative process I see it as a search for the 'right' word or image *in* which the depth dimension shines up.

In conclusion I should like to quote a good example of the way in which O'Connor handles complex images and how she uses them to make them translucent for the depth dimension that she is always trying to keep the reader aware of. Mrs. Flood, who had so far not been able to see beyond the literal, has the following 'tunnel-vision' when she sees the dead Hazel Motes at the end of *Wise Blood*:

The deep burned eye sockets seemed to lead into the dark tunnel where he had disappeared. … She shut her eyes and saw the pin point of light but so far away that she could not hold it steady in her mind. She felt as if she were blocked at the entrance of something. She sat staring with her eyes shut, into his eyes, and she felt as if she had finally got to the beginning of something she couldn't begin, and she saw him moving farther and farther away, farther and farther into the darkness until he was the pin point of light.

Chapter 2

O'Connor's Artistic Development

EXEMPLIFIED THROUGH THE 'JUDGEMENT-DAY' MATERIAL

In many ways 'Judgement Day' holds a unique position in Flannery O'Connor's oeuvre. Very early in her career she presented the material in 'The Geranium', which was her first story ever to be published *(Accent*, vol. VI, Summer 1946) and which she made the opening story of her master's thesis, submitted in June 1947. Late in 1954 she had another go at the material and rewrote it into 'An Exile in the East', which she sent to Elizabeth McKee on January 13, 1955: 'The carbon of "An Exile in the East" is enclosed, but I don't know if you realize or not that this is a rewritten version of "The Geranium" originally printed in *Accent. Accent* didn't pay me for it and it is rather much changed, but I enclose both stories so [the editor] can see what she's doing. I don't want to go to the penitentiary for selling a story twice (but if I do I would like to get a good price for the story)' (HB 74-75). But in June she wrote: 'Also you have a copy of a story called "An Exile in the East"[1] that they didn't put in the collection.[2] Please send this back to me and in my spare time I may give it a shot of ACTH[3] and send it back in some better shape'.[4] In her very last phase Flannery O'Connor returned to the material once again and in a letter[5] to Giroux about her plans for the new collection *Everything That Rises Must Converge* she remarks: 'There is a story that I have been working on off and on for several years that I may be able to finish in time to include'.[6] Twenty days before her

---

1 It was published posthumously by Jan Nordby Gretlund in *The South Carolina Review* vol. 11, Nov. 1978, 12-21 and in *The Best American Short Stories* 1979, ed. Joyce Carol Oates, 28-38.
2 I.e. *A Good Man Is Hard to Find*.
3 The medicine she used against her disease.
4 HB 88. There is manuscript evidence – Dunn 193 – that Flannery O'Connor wanted to include 'An Exile in the East' in the collection *A Good Man Is Hard to Find*, but after finishing 'Good Country People' she decided to use the latter instead.
5 Dated May 21, 1964, HB 579.
6 HB 579-80. The story O'Connor here talks about is 'Judgement Day'.

death she finds that the story is now so different from 'The Geranium' that 'I am to sell it again' (HB 594). In her letter to C. Carver of June 17, 1964 she says: 'I've got one [Judgement Day] that I'm not satisfied with that I finished about the same time as "Revelation"' (HB 585), which must have been towards the end of November 1963, since she wrote to M. Lee on November 29, 'I have writ a story [Revelation] with which I am, for the time anyway, pleased pleased pleased' (HB 551). On June 28 she 'completed' it, but wanted 'to keep it a few weeks longer and think about it' (HB 589). When she started her final rewriting of the story, she called it 'Getting Home' – in the collection of manuscripts Dunn 194a, 194b, 194c, but in 194d she crossed out 'Getting Home' and replaced it by the published title 'Judgement Day'.[7] This story and 'Parker's Back' are the last material on which Flannery O'Connor worked during her final weeks and days and they could therefore justly be called her testament.

In the O'Connor manuscript Collection in Milledgeville there is only one full-length manuscript of 'The Geranium' (Dunn 12 d), a working draft (Dunn 12 c) and two three-page fragments (Dunn 12 a, b). In Dunn 12 b and c, O'Connor makes Old Dudley jump out of the window to pick up the geranium. This version would have clearly underlined the parallel of uprootedness between Old Dudley and the geranium. There is no hint why O'Connor scrapped this version in favor of the much less conclusive ending of the published story with the owner's threat '"I only tell people once"' (CS 14) hovering in the air.

The collection holds only one 16-page manuscript of 'An Exile in the East' (Dunn 193). The final version of the material is represented with no less than twenty-one manuscripts: Dunn 194 a,b,c,d; 195 a,b,c,d,e,f,g,h; 196 a,b,c,d,e,f,g; and 197a,b. 197a, called 'Judgment [sic] Day' is the 25-page manuscript of the published version. 197b is a carbon copy of 197a, which C. Carver had returned with comments to O'Connor by July 15, 1964 (HB 593) and which O'Connor used for last minute corrections. This shows how seriously she worked to get the final version right. There are no less than ten different versions of the ending of the story.

---

7 Flannery O'Connor may have been induced to this new title by Tanner's exclamation 'Judgement Day' (Cf. *Flannery O'Connor, The Complete Stories*, New York, 1980, 549), which occurs for the first time in the Dunn 194b, c, and d versions, p. 26. 194c and d are carbon copies of 194b.

In 'An Exile in the East' the protagonist has acquired a new name, Old Tanner, which he will retain in 'Judgement Day' after his early manuscript identity of 'Franklyn Turner Fairlee'.[8] In keeping with the two parts of the title 'An Exile in the East' the East is dramatized in greater – negative – detail. The son-in-law comes alive with 'his nasel [*sic*] yankee whisper' calling Tanner 'the cotton bale'.[9] The characteristic O'Connor tone has found its way into the story: 'His daughter wouldn't let him wear his hat inside except when he sat like this in front of the window. He told her it was necessary to keep the light out of his eyes; which it was not: the light here was as weak as everything else' (Dunn 193 p. 2). There is a rather noisy introduction to the next-door neighbor whom Tanner hears rent the flat. 'Outside a woman shrieked something unintelligible and a garbage can fell on one of the fire escapes and banged to the concrete. Then inside, the door to the next apartment slammed and he heard a sharp distinct footstep clip down the hall'.[10] Tanner hates him from the beginning although the black neighbor is drawn even more sympathetically than in 'The Geranium'. Tanner lacks physical strength much more than in 'The Geranium'. Therefore the entire New York outing (CS 7) with his daughter is cut to her asking him to go for a stroll. 'A stroll. He could barely manage to stay upright on his feet and she used the word *stroll*' (Dunn 193 p. 3). Similarly, when Tanner is asked to go down to Mrs Smith, he 'moved off, watching his feet under him as if they were two small children he was encouraging to get out of his way' (Dunn 193 p. 12). We learn more about the Tanner family background: 'He had raised up five boys and this girl with sawmilling and farming …' (Dunn 193 p. 4). Tanner hates his daughter's dutifulness even more: '… she was hog-wild. She was thirsting for some duty to do, … She had shivered all over with duty' (Dunn 193 p. 4). A postcard from Coleman, who in this version replaces Rabie et al. and one from Tanner to Coleman underline Tanner's forty-year acquaintance with Coleman, as does Tanner's first meeting

---

8 Dunn 194b; 195g,h; 196b,c,d,e,f,g; 197a.

9 Dunn 193 p. 1. Later in the story Tanner thinks of himself in the same way: 'There were two trickles of water running over his tight cheeks and he leaned farther forward and let them fall on the steps as if his head were a pitcher he was emptying. Then he began to move on up the steps, like a cotton bale with short legs and a black hat'. p. 15.

10 Ibid. p. 9. A comparison with the passage in the published version (CS 7-8) shows how much more concrete the 'Exile' version is.

with Coleman, who is much more fully drawn here than in the later 'Judgement Day' text. Accordingly, Tanner's longing for the South grows stronger: 'He would probably be dead by the time he got half-way there but it would be better to be dead halfway home than to be living here' (Dunn 193 p. 11). Tanner makes several plans to escape from his exile. In one of them 'he had imagined that he would pretend he was dead and have his body shipped back and when he arrived he would knock on the inside of the box and they would let him out. Cole-man would stand there with his red eyeballs starting out and think he had rose from the dead' (Dunn 193 p. 13). Here we have the first indi-cation that the South means more than simply getting home.

To sum up: 'The Geranium' is a third-person narrative, set in New York, with little dialogue. Old Dudley feels out of place there as does the flower he sees in the window across the street. With some ease we move in and out of Dudley's mind, but there are only two short drama-tized memories of Dudley's past in the South, i.e. his fishing and hunt-ing with Rabie (CS 5; 11-12). But there is no vision of the future. Old Dudley feels 'his throat knotting up' and he weeps. He is frightened and isolated in a hostile environment, but he does nothing about his situ-ation, despite the fact that he is not as near death as he is in the later ver-sions. Old Dudley romanticizes his past in the South as opposed to his present in New York where 'people boiled out of trains'. There is next to no distancing irony, and at the end the reader is left with the mor-bid impression that Old Dudley might end up as his displaced friend, the geranium, 'roots in the air', also in the concrete sense.

'An Exile in the East' is also a third-person narrative, but whenever we leave the narrator's mind – and we do so with greater ease than in 'The Geranium' – we encounter episodes with dialogue from Tanner's past, present and future. The dreaming about the South is replaced by dramatized narrative. The style with its detached irony is much more O'Connor's trademark. Thanks to the dramatizations also the minor characters come alive. Tanner feels his isolation and humiliation much more, and though weaker, he is making plans for a journey home. In this connection I see the addition of the story about Tanner's imagined death as an essentially new venture. Home is no longer an idealized South, it is the safe haven to be reached after death. Similarly, the 'here' or New York of the story also symbolizes man's ambience before death. However, the story ends in almost the same way as 'The Geranium', and this may have induced O'Connor to further re-writings.

The 'Getting Home' version shows many signs of stylistic polishing, and O'Connor reaches here some of the happy formulations that she kept in the final version. There is Old Fairlee's confession: 'He would have been a nigger's white nigger any day'.[11] It is in this version that O'Connor lets the daughter live in 'a pigeon-hutch of a building'.[12] But Flannery O'Connor does not seem to have been sure about the ending. In Dunn 194b, which is a full-length manuscript of this version but to which she added a hand-written note saying 'Not for publication',[13] she ends the story with a discussion between daughter and husband, in which the daughter convinces him that the old man must be buried in the South. This is crossed out in Dunn 194d and replaced by the version we know from 'Judgement Day' (CS 550), but the last subordinate clause runs, 'which at her time of life is essential' (Dunn 194d p. 27). O'Connor must have noticed the unfortunate transition from the third-person point-of-view in 'Now she rests well at night' to the authorial comment 'which at her time of life is essential'. It needed many revisions before the perfect formulation with the obligatory O'Connor irony was reached in 'and her good looks have mostly returned'.

In this version the next-door black resident is identified further. He becomes the 'nigger-actor' (Dunn 194b p. 16), and the sympathetic character traits O'Connor had given him in 'An Exile in the East' are dropped; thus it is more convincing that he slams Old Fairlee against the wall and finally kills him. Now it is Old Fairlee who desperately tries to get in contact with him. In the dramatization of Old Fairlee's journey to the South we read, '"Judgment [*sic*] Day!" he cried, sitting up in the box and catching hold of Coleman's coat' (Dunn 194b p. 26). This is the first occurrence of the later title in the entire manuscript material. Not surprisingly so, since one of the two distinctive additions in Dunn 194b to the material as we know it up to 'An Exile in the East' is the mentioning of biblical references. This may also have induced O'Connor to change the title 'Getting Home' to the final 'Judgement Day'. Jesus is mentioned early in this version,[14] later Old Fairlee asks for the daughter's Bible,[15] and there is a long passage[16] where father and daughter talk about death and hell, in the course of which the old man

---

11 Dunn 194b p. 13. Cf. CS 540.
12 Dunn 194d p. 15. Cf. CS 541.
13 Dunn 194h, p. 1.
14 Dunn 194a, p. 5, 194 b, p. 5.
15 Dunn 194b, p. 14; also 195e, p. 14; 195f, p. 21.
16 Dunn 194b, pp. 21, 23, 24.

asks "'What did Jesus do?'" (Dunn 194b p. 93) His daughter explains that he was crucified but rose from the dead; but that she does not believe in any of it. O'Connor must have found that these references made the story much less ambivalent. Consequently she crossed out those pages in Dunn 194d, a carbon copy of 194b. The only reminiscences of these direct references to the Bible that found their way into the published version are the actor's remarks: "'And I'm not no preacher! I'm not even no Christian. I don't believe in that crap. There ain't no Jesus and there ain't no God'" (CS 545). The other essential addition in the 'Getting Home' version is the figure of Dr. Foley.[17] 'He was only part black. The rest was white and Indian' (Dunn 194b p. 7). In Dunn 194d O'Connor made him 'part Jew' but already in Dunn 195c p. 6 this was erased in favor of the final 'The rest was Indian and white' (CS 535). Old Fairlee's meeting with Foley is here as in the 'Judgement Day' versions the frame around the flashback about Old Fairlee's first meeting with Coleman, whom he had on his hands 'for thirty years' (Dunn 194b, p. 12), not forty as in the 'An Exile in the East' version (Dunn 193 p. 6). One other change is important: whereas the story so far was set in the summer: 'They set it out and let the hot sun bake it all day' (CS 3) we read in 'The Geranium'. New York is now snow-clad: 'The window ledge across the street was covered with snow'.[18] With this change O'Connor brought the setting in line with the heavy emphasis on death in the final version. Old Fairlee's resolution to get home is firm in spite of the weather.

Also, in the last 'Getting Home' manuscript O'Connor changed Old Fairlee's name to Tanner, though not consistently so.[19] The Dunn 195 fragments prove that O'Connor was uncertain about keeping or striking the references to the Bible;[20] she decided against them in the end. The most interesting feature of these fragments is the new endings. Here the daughter keeps her promise and sees to it that Tanner is buried in the South.[21] All along there are small stylistic improvements which bring the manuscripts closer to the published version, which pulls together most of the earlier strings.

---

17 Dunn 194b, pp. 7, 12.

18 Dunn 194a, p 4; and it is snowing outside 194b, p. 23.

19 Dunn 194d, p. 4.

20 In Dunn 195e, p. 14 the Bible discussion is kept; in 195f, p. 20 Tanner's thoughts about death are crossed out, but on p. 21 the Bible references are kept.

21 Dunn 195h, p. 26; 196f, p. 26; 196g, pp. 26-7.

All the more surprising was it for me to discover through manuscript comparison that the published version of 'Judgement Day' does not seem to be based on Flannery O'Connor's final revisions. The published text is based on the version of Dunn 197a[22] whereas Flannery's final emendations are found in Dunn 197b.

Why did that happen, why were Flannery's last-minute changes not honored by the editors? I asked Sally Fitzgerald whether she had any explanation. In her letter of July 15, 1982, she writes, in case my findings hold true, 'I feel sure that the corrected version never reached Giroux. It might not have occurred to Mrs. O'Connor to send it along, so it just fetched up with the papers'. Probably we shall never come closer to the correct answer.

In the following I try to describe the manuscript evidence, then go through the major differences between the published text and the manuscript Dunn 197b, and finally assess how the last changes affect the story as a whole.[23]

MANUSCRIPT EVIDENCE

In the present context we can concentrate on the 'Judgement Day' manuscripts 197a and 197b. 197b is clearly a carbon copy of 197a, both comprising pages 1-25, entitled 'Judgment [sic] Day'. Flannery O'Connor worked on the typed text with black ink and with her typewriter. On p. 15 Tanner originally signed his postcard to Coleman: 'Yours truly, Franklyn Turner'.[24] Flannery struck 'Franklyn' and typed it 'W.T'. and

---

22 Except for editorial respellings and Tanner's remark in CS 533: '"You promised you'd bury me there."' With no authority in Dunn 194a, which is the manuscript basis for the published text, p. 4, the posthumous editors – quite in keeping with the context – replaced 'there' for the manuscript's 'here'. Flannery corrected the mistake in 197b!

23 In *Flannery O'Connor: The Growing Craft* I have given detailed analyses of Flannery O'Connor's artistic development and her changing focus in the many versions of 'The Geranium'/'Judgement Day'.

24 In 'An Exile in the East' the Old Dudley of 'The Geranium' is called Tanner. In the early versions of 'Judgement Day' Flannery called the character Franklyn Turner Fairlee, F.T. Fairlee or Old Fairlee – cf. Dunn 194a, b, c. In 194d Flannery O'Connor started replacing F.T. Fairlee by 'Tanner' but kept the name on the postcard. The Dunn 195 and 196 manuscripts show some vacillation between the use of Fairlee and Tanner. Manuscripts 197a and 197b show Tanner throughout except for the instance mentioned here.

'Turner' became 'Tanner'.[25] On p. 17 the original typescript runs: 'He was willing to bet the nigger would like to talk about home to someone who understood him' (CS 543). With black ink Flannery deleted 'about home', thus adding much deeper dimensions to the sentence. In another instance – p. 19 – the original runs: 'The rest of the day he sat in his chair and debated whether he would have one more try at being friendly to the negro'. With black ink Flannery cut out the last five words and replaced them with the much more personal 'making friends with him' (CS 545).

The changes that Flannery O'Connor made in 197a are also to be found in 197b. The following example shows clearly that she transferred the changes in 197a to 197b – and not *vice versa*. She had some trouble with the very last sentence of the story. Originally she had written 'Now she rests well at night, ...'[26] then crossed out 'well at', added in handwriting 'she sleeps' which is again deleted and replaced in handwriting by the original 'well at'. None of these corrections in 197a occur in 197b, where the original is left untouched.

Apart from Flannery's corrections, which are identical in 197a and 197b, 197b shows light blue pencil marks in the text and in the margin, clearly not Flannery's own, and changes in black pencil from Flannery's hand. Some of the changes are clearly the author's reaction to the blue pencil queries; others are spontaneous. The fact that Flannery in the 197b manuscript even made some changes in the corrections transferred to 197b from 197a proves beyond doubt, I think, that 197b is later and therefore *the* final version of 'Judgement Day'. I shall discuss the details later.

The next question is, whose are the blue pencil suggestions? And does a satisfying answer to this question add to the evidence that Dunn 197b is the final version of 'Judgement Day'? Here Flannery O'Connor's letters help. On June 17, 1964, she writes to Catherine Carver:[27] 'I've got one ["Judgement Day"] that I'm not satisfied with that I finished about the same time as "Revelation" and when I get home I'm going to send it to you as is, and ask you to let me know what you think of

---

25 A highly appropriate emendation, I think, for a Tanner would not use his first names in a message to Coleman. Why O'Connor initialed Tanner 'W.T.' here and 'T.C.' at the opening of the story (CS 531; Dunn 197a and b, p. 1) I do not know.

26 CS 550, Dunn 197a and b, p. 25.

27 Ever since Catherine Carver had become Flannery O'Connor's editor at Harcourt, Brace and Company in 1955 – cf. HB 76-77 – Flannery trusted her judgment and she often sent manuscripts to Carver for comments.

it' (HB 585). This she did on June 27, and in her covering letter she writes: 'Will you look at this one ["Judgement Day"] and say if you think it fitten [*sic*] for the collection or if you think it can be made so? It's a rewrite of a story that I have had around since 1946 and never satisfied with, but I hope I have it now except for details maybe' (HB 588). Notice that Flannery invites general comments and that she leaves Catherine Carver the opportunity to suggest 'details' that may be changed.

On the following day she wrote to Giroux: 'I've completed one story ["Judgement Day"] which I think will do in place of "The Partridge Festival." But I want to keep it a few weeks longer and think about it before I send it' (HB 589). Think about it she did; send it she never could.

Catherine Carver worked fast, and on July 15 Flannery could write back to her: 'I do thank you and I'll get to work on this one ["Judgement Day"] you sent back. I can see the point about the daughter's coming being too close to his encounter with the doctor. As for the "on his back" business – that's a cherished Southern white assertion – that the Negro *is* on his back and in a way it's quite true' (HB 593). Notice that Flannery will 'get to work on this one'. Do we find evidence in 197b of the two points she comments on in her letter? Yes.

On p. 6 in 197b Catherine Carver put an X in the margin and underlined 'same' in 'that same afternoon he had found out different' (CS 535). Flannery changed the manuscript accordingly and struck the following passage:

That same afternoon he had found out different. He had found out in time to go back with her. If he had found out a day later, he might still be there, squatting on the doctor's land.

When he saw the brown porpoise-shaped figure striding across the field that afternoon, he had known at once what had happened.

The final version according to 197b runs:

He should have known different. Later in the summer when he saw the brown porpoise-shaped figure striding across the field, he knew at once what had happened.

As Flannery indicated in her letter, she did not accept Carver's queries about 'on his back'. On p. 8 of 197b Carver had put an encircled ? and a vertical stroke in the margin and underlined in the text as follows: '*Then* he would jump *on your back* and know he had a good thing there for life' (CS 536). But, quite in keeping with the letter, Flannery O'Connor did not change the manuscript here.

By now I hope to have proved that Dunn 197b *is* the Catherine Carver copy[28] and that it contains Flannery O'Connor's final changes in the text of 'Judgement Day'. Despite the fact that there is no indication in the manuscript or otherwise that Flannery intended this version for publication, Dunn 197b is the last version and should therefore have been published, since she herself did not send 197a to Giroux and since she had suggested to Carver that she was willing to change details in the version – identical with 197a – she had sent to her. I suggest that the publishers honor the work that Flannery painfully accomplished in her last days – the corrections in Dunn 197b were made between July 15 and the day of her death and the corrections show how weak her hand was – and in future editions of 'Judgement Day' use the final version.

THE PUBLISHED TEXT AND DUNN 197B

Since the final version is not fully available in print, I shall try to communicate an impression of the energy that Flannery O'Connor used for these last corrections of the text. Catherine Carver's blue pencil made a total of 29 marks in the text and 39 in the margin, but Flannery's changes are much more numerous. The major changes are given below; no corrections in spelling or punctuation are included. Page numbers in front of the quotations refer to *Complete Stories*, page references to Dunn 197b are indicated after the quote. Changes prompted by Catherine Carver are marked with (CC). The actual changes are italicized in the quotation.

---

28 Further evidence for the fact that the light blue pencil marks come from Catherine Carver's hand is found in the Dunn 189b manuscript of 'Revelation'. Here we find the same pencil and the same symbols used in the margin and the text. On December 6, 1963, O'Connor wrote to 'A' that she had sent a copy of this story to Carver, but that she had not heard from her yet. (HB 552) But in her Christmas letter to 'A' (December 25, 1963) she writes: 'Yes mam I heard from C. Carver. … She thought it ['Revelation'] one of my most powerful stories and probably my blackest. Found Ruby evil. Found end vision to confirm same. Though suggested I leave it out. I am not going to leave it out. I am going to deepen it so that there'll be no mistaking Ruby is not just an evil Glad Annie'. (HB 554) Dunn 189d proves that Flannery took Carver's suggestions seriously. This manuscript is changed according to Carver's suggestions in 189b.

p. 531 'He couldn't *leave* until she got out of the way'. (p. 1)

p. 532 '*Dead or alive. It was being there that mattered; the dead or alive did not*.' (deleted on p. 2; CC)

p. 532 '*He heard her say,* "You ought to get you a hat."' (p. 2)

p. 532 "And sit all day in it", the son-in-law said, "like him in there. *Yah!*" (deleted on p. 2)

p. 532 'The son-in-law had a stupid muscular face and *a* yankee voice to go with it'. (p. 3)

p. 532 'He never worked for nobody in his life but himself, and *he* had people – other people – working for him'. (p. 3; CC)

p. 532 "Yah so I don't have brains," the son-in-law said'.

p. 533 "You got them," she said. "You don't always use them.""

'One of the sudden very occasional, feelings of warmth for the daughter came over Tanner. Every now and then she said something that might make you think she had a little sense stored away somewhere for safe keeping'.

"*He didn't have the brains to hang on to what he did have,*" *the son-in-law said,* "*and she tells me he can handle a …*""

"He has a stroke when he sees a nigger in the building." *the son-in-law said*'. ('the son-in-law said' deleted on p. 3)

p. 533 "*Bury who?*"' (deleted on p. 3) "*Him in there.*"' (deleted on p. 4)

p. 533 "I'm not taking that trip down there again with *any body*."

"You stick to your guns," he said. "*Yah. Well* I just wanted to make sure." *he said*'. (p. 4. 'Yah. Well' and 'he said' are deleted.)

p. 533 'When she returned to the room, Tanner had *had* both hands gripped on the chair arms'. (p. 4)

p. 533 "You promised you'd bury me *t*here."' (p. 4; CC had suggested insertion of 'not' after 'you'd'. Cf. also note no. 22.)

p. 533 'Still the tears *ran* down his cheeks;' (p. 4)

p. 534 'there was nobody left who felt a duty toward him but her, married and childless, in New York City like Mrs. Big. *and ready when she came back and found him living the way he was to take him back with her*'. (deleted on p. 5)

'*After he had left the place*[29] *she had come down in person to offer him a home with her. The son-in-law brought her and leaned against a tree with a*

---

29 Presumably a reference to Tanner's earlier family home. This change was prompted by Carver's margin remark 'Why?' and explains 'Mrs. Big's' trip to the South. Also a stroke in the margin on p. 12 contributed to Flannery's clarifying changes here.

cigaret hanging out of his mouth. He never said a word but hello. She had put her face ...' (p. 5; CC)

p. 534 'The daughter stepped back onto the *ground.* The bottoms of two cane chairs were tilted against the *side of the shack* but she declined to take a seat. She stepped out about ten feet as if it took that much space to clear the odor. Then she *spoke* her piece'. (p. 5)

p. 534 "My mother raised me to do it." "*if you didn't*" (deleted on p. 6)

p. 534 'At that point *Coleman* roused up ...' (p. 6)

p. 535 '*She had shamed him.* (deleted) He shouted so both *she and Coleman* could hear'. (p. 6)

p. 535 "'That *no-good* scoundrel has been on my hands for thirty years."' ('no-good' deleted on p. 6)

p. 535 "'*You go on back up there. I wouldn't come with you for no million dollars or no sack of salt.*"

"It looks like you and him built it. Whose land is it on?"' (deleted on p. 6)

"'Whose land is it?" *she persisted*'. (p. 6)

p. 535 For Flannery O'Connor's change of the time sequence see my comments above in connection with note 18 and p. 52.

p. 536 "'Ain't been your property long," *Tanner* said'. (p. 7)

p. 536 "'I never found nothing that paid yet," *Tanner* muttered'. (p. 8)

p. 537 '*Tanner* had ignored him for a day ...'(p. 9)

p. 539 'He stopped in the middle of the yard, *about where the day before the daughter had delivered her ultimatum*'. (deleted on p. 12; CC's comment in the margin was 'scrap day p. 6'.)

p. 540 "'If you want to run the still for me, that's one thing," the doctor said. "If you don't you might as well *had* be packing up"'. (deleted on p. 12)

p. 540 "'*I don't have to work for you,*" he said'. (deleted on p. 12)

"'The governmint ain't got around yet to forcing the white folks to work for the colored," *Tanner said*'. (p. 12)

p. 540 'Tanner's gaze drove past the farthest blue edge of the tree line into the pale *empty* afternoon sky'. (deleted on p. 13)

p. 540 'He appeared to have measured and to know secretly the time it would take *the world* to *turn* upside down'. (p. 13)

Carver had drawn attention to the passage: 'The negro laughed softly. "Down on you luck, ain't you?" he murmured. "Didn't you used to own a little piece of land over acrost the river and lost it?"' (CS 539)

p. 540 "'The black ones they *rears* and they pitches.'" (p. 13; CC)

p. 540 "'I be back here next week,' he said, "and if you still here, I know you going to work *that still* for me.'" (p. 13)

p. 541 'His heart *beat faster*. He heard her plump herself down on the sofa'. (p. 14)

p. 542 'After a while a large negro in a light *blue suit came lunging up the stairs, carrying four bulging* canvas suitcases, his head lowered against the strain'. (p. 16)

p. 543 "'And got him his high-yeller, high-stepping woman with *a* red *wig* and they two are going to live next door to you!'" (p. 17)

p. 543 'A real sweal [*sic*]. *The negro* came on without appearing to see there was anyone else in the hall'. (p. 17)

p. 544 'Once in the middle of the afternoon, he caught the negro's eye, *or thought he did,* just as he was rounding the bend of the stairs again…' (p. 18)

p. 544 'The negro came out about *ten* o'clock'. (p. 18)

p. 544 "'I thought you might know somewhere around here we could find us a pond *and fish,* Preacher, …'" (p. 19; CC)

p. 545 "'And I'm not *a* Preacher! I'm an actor.'" (p. 19; CC)

p. 545 "'Good evening, Preacher,' he said. *forgetting that the negro called himself an actor'.* (last part deleted on p. 19)

p. 545 "'And I'm not *a* preacher! I'm not *a* Christian. …'" (p. 19)

p. 545 'From the kitchen the daughter saw him blindly hit the edge of the inside hall door and fall reeling into the *living* room'. (deleted on p. 20)
    'Hard as his head, the fall cracked it and when he got over the concussion he had a little stroke*. For days his tongue appeared to be frozen in his mouth'. (p. 20; CC)

p. 545 'What he wanted to know was if the government check had come. He meant to buy a bus ticket with it and go home. After a few *weeks,* he made her understand'. (p. 20)

p. 546 'It had come to him then slowly just what his present situation was. *He would never see Corinth again.* At least he would have to make her understand that he must be sent home to be buried'. (p. 20)

Near the bottom of p. 20 Catherine Carver had asked in the margin: 'some dialogue here?' Flannery O'Connor agreed and made the following passage more dramatic by adding pieces of dialogue.

p. 546 'Coleman would do the rest'.
    "'*I'm not letting the nigger bury you,*" she said, "*but quit being morbid. You'll be up and around in a while.*'"[30]

'After a lot of argument, he wrung the promise from her. She would ship him back. *It had only been, he saw now, to shut him up.*'

'After that he slept peacefully and improved a little. In his *waking* dreams he could feel the cold early morning air of home coming in through the cracks of the pine box'. (p. 20)

p. 546 'He *saw* Coleman waiting, red-eyed, on the station platform and Hooten standing there with his green eyeshade and black alpaca sleeves, *waiting for the train to stop. Hooten would be thinking:* If the old fool had stayed at home where he belonged, he wouldn't be arriving on the 6:03 in no box. Coleman *would turn* the borrowed mule...' (p. 21)

p. 546 '*Everything was ready*' (deleted on p. 21) '*When the coffin was off the train* the two of them, shut-mouthed, *would inch* the loaded coffin toward the wagon. From inside he *would begin* to scratch on the wood. They *would drop the box* as if it had caught fire'. (p. 21)

p. 546 '"That him," Coleman would *say.* "He in there his self."

"Naw," Hooten *would say,* "must be a rat got in there with him."' (p. 21)

p. 546 'Hooten *would go* grumbling and *get* the crowbar and *come* back and *begin* to pry open the lid. Even before he had the upper end pried open, Coleman *would be* jumping up and down, wheezing and panting from excitement. Tanner *would give* a thrust. *upward with both hands and sprang up in the box*'. (last part of sentence deleted on p. 21)

'"Judgement Day! Judgement Day!" he *would cry.*' (p. 21)

Prompted by Catherine Carver, Flannery O'Connor wrote 'space' above the following sentence to indicate that it should be set off more clearly from the previous 'dream' passage:

p. 547 'Now *that* he knew exactly what her promises were worth'. (p. 21; CC)

p. 547 'This was the last time he would see her flat dumb face. *Then* he felt guilty'. (p. 22)

p. 547 '"It was my fault trying to be friendly with that *city* nigger." And I'm a damned liar besides, he said to himself to kill the *outrageous* (deleted) taste such a statement made in his mouth'. (p. 22)

p. 547 '"It's great to have you here," she said *in return*'. (p. 22)

p. 549 '"*He in there*," Coleman said, "one of his tricks."' (p. 24)

p. 549 '"Oh," Tanner *murmured,* "it's you."' (p. 25)

p. 549 '"*There's not any* judgement day, old man. *Except* this."' (p. 25; CC)

---

30 Flannery forgot about direct speech punctuation here.

HOW DO THE FINAL CHANGES AFFECT THE STORY AS A WHOLE?

Considering the fact that Flannery O'Connor had worked on the shape of this material from the beginning of her career, it is certainly amazing that she was willing and able to make so many changes even in her last days. If nothing else, this proves her untiring dedication to her art. The result was a much better version than the one we now have in *The Complete Stories*. One might be tempted to discard the many revisions of the same material as a lack of imagination, but I suggest that we consider them as an indication of the central position this material holds in O'Connor's universe, indicative of Flannery O'Connor's development as artist and thinker. Some remarks about the first paragraph of the published version of 'Judgement Day' will have to suffice to show O'Connor's perfect economy of style.

In spite of his weakness (CS 534)[31] Tanner is entirely in charge; he will make his trip home, trusting only in himself for the first part of the trip and in the Almighty for the rest. 'He had allowed his daughter to dress him' (CS 531). 'Today' he will escape from a New York, which is even less charming than in the earlier versions 'an alley full of New York air, the kind fit for cats and garbage' (CS 531). He will escape in spite of the snow and the growing cold 'the snow was beginning to stick and freeze to the outside pane' (CS 547). The narrated time comprises only a few hours and the story is told as a third-person narrative, restricted almost entirely to Tanner's point of view. Seamlessly we move with him from his present to flashbacks and flash forwards. This point-of-view technique leads O'Connor to the externalization of the daughter's interior duologue, interspersed with Tanner's comments. 'Her voice rose from the kitchen. "As bad as having a child. He wanted to come and now he's here, he don't like it." He had not wanted to come. "Pretended he didn't but I could tell"' (CS 533-34). The story starts in the present with Tanner's eavesdropping on his daughter's talking to herself and to her husband. After a short tête-à-tête with his daughter about her promise to bury him in the South, we move into the past. 'She had put her face in the door of the shack and had stared, expres-

---

31 Now also his vision is failing and he is paralysed by a stroke. 'He controlled one hand by holding the other on top of it'. 'All he had to do was push one foot in front of the other' (CS 531-32).

sionless, for a second' (CS 534). This flashback leads to the Dr. Foley flashback, only a few hours less remote in the past. 'He had found out in time to go back with her. If he had found out a day later, he might still be there, squatting on the doctor's land. When he saw the brown porpoise-shaped figure striding across the field that afternoon, he had known at once what had happened' (CS 535). This again glides brilliantly over into the distant past and Tanner's first meeting with Coleman. 'He had had Coleman on his back for thirty years. Tanner had first seen Coleman when he was working six of them' (CS 536). From this account we move smoothly back into the Foley story (CS 539) from which we are led back into Tanner's New York present with his daughter (CS 540), who tries to cheer him up and make him 'quit thinking about morbid stuff, death and hell and judgement' (CS 541). With a fine touch of tragic irony O'Connor lets Tanner answer, "'The Judgement (CS 535)[32] is coming'" (CS 541). Here Tanner is thinking of Judgment Day in general, but is not aware of his own personal judgment, with which he will be faced that same day. After Tanner's musing about Coleman's imagined visit to New York we are in the immediate past and Tanner's confrontation with the actor, which shows Tanner utterly out of touch with the reality of his situation. Disillusioned more than ever, we hear him tell his daughter about his plans to leave. Once she has promised him that 'she would ship him back' (CS 546), he can sleep peacefully and in this sleep he experiences his flash forward about his trip to the South in the box. 'He could feel the cold early morning air of home coming in through the cracks of the pine box' (CS 546). Back in the present for a final meeting with his daughter, Tanner is on his way. The last movements between present and future and back to the present are almost unnoticeable. O'Connor is technically at her best here: 'He landed upside down in the middle of the flight. He felt presently the tilt of the box as they took it off the train. ... "Coleman?" he murmured. The negro bending over him had a large surly mouth and sullen eyes. "Ain't any coal man, either," he said' (CS 548-49). When Tanner realizes that he has muddled up the future and the present, he asks the actor "'Hep me up, Preacher. I'm on my way home!'" (CS 549) And the actor sends him home in many a sense of that word.

---

32 Notice the capital J against the daughter's small j.

To sum up: after many revisions 'Judgement Day' is not only perfect in style and structure, also the characters are fully drawn: Tanner shows concern for Coleman and for his daughter and vice versa. And the message has reached new dimensions: the longing for the South of 'The Geranium' has been activated and spiritualized. Tanner is no longer nostalgically longing for his home in the South, which wasn't so perfect, after all; he really makes an effort to get home, but home not only means safety, warmth and understanding, it is the final goal of life to which death is the door. His journey is life's journey. Tanner is prepared for that journey, he has reached self-recognition, he has shown concern for others, and he has given himself over into the hands of the Almighty. However, the moment of judgment reaches him unawares, as it does many of his fellow O'Connor characters and from an entirely unexpected source.

Granted, most of the changes are minor details, but they all help to clarify the author's meaning and to improve the story technically. Some corrections, however, add substantially to the body of the narrative. By giving a reason for the daughter's original visit with Tanner and by placing this visit 'later in the summer' the account of Tanner's meeting with Foley and with his daughter *cum* son-in-law gains greater verisimilitude and consistency. In similar manner, Flannery O'Connor underlines the dream character of Tanner's imagined trip in the coffin by replacing the original simple verb forms with composite forms, where the auxiliary 'would' emphasizes the counterfactuality of the statements. In this way, Tanner's 'waking' dream is set off more distinctly against the surrounding passages.

By rearranging the discussion between Tanner's daughter and son-in-law and by allowing the son-in-law an extra remark, the conflict between Tanner and his son-in-law gains effect, and the son-in-law's character becomes more colorful. In keeping with this is the more detailed description of the daughter's visit to the South (CS 534).

Also the daughter's relation to Tanner is changed. She shows much more concern for him in the final version. She does not shame him (CS 535), and she doesn't attack him for having neglected his duties as an educator (CS 534). Flannery also scrapped the remark about the daughter's 'ultimatum' (CS 539). After Tanner's stroke the daughter promises that she will bury him, and she gives him new hope (CS 546), though Tanner does not believe in the sincerity of her statement.

The final version also shows greater vividness and consistency in the depiction of the 'city nigger' and his woman, who becomes even less attractive in her red wig, and the physicality of the man is underlined by the fact that he carries 'four bulging' canvas suitcases (CS 542-43). And certainly prompted by her ever-present irony, Flannery made the black man leave his flat at 'ten' and not at eight o'clock. After all, he was an actor. Tanner's first physical confrontation with the black actor is rendered much more brutally (CS 545), which also explains his ensuing weakness. Flannery O'Connor also polished his language. As an actor and a 'city nigger' of 'uppity' inclinations, he would not use double negations. Therefore: "'I'm not a preacher! I'm not a Christian'"(CS 545). Similarly the much more polished "'There's not any judgement day, old man. Except this'"(CS 549), which at the same time sets the 'city nigger's' language off against Coleman's.

Characteristic of Flannery O'Connor's conscientious use of 'the right word' is the deletion of the much too strong 'flooded' (CS 533) in favor of the much calmer and more realistic 'ran'. Therefore, she also struck the pleonastic epithet 'no-good' in connection with the word 'scoundrel' (CS 535). She sensed the clash in the 'pale empty afternoon sky' (CS 540) and cut out 'empty'. In the final version she lets Tanner's heart 'beat faster' (CS 541) instead of the wrong emphasis of the earlier 'accelerated'. Along the same lines is her deletion of 'outrageous' (CS 547), which was an entirely inappropriate description of 'the taste such a statement made in his mouth'.

Finally, there are the two words which surely puzzled the editors. What meaning could they possibly make of 'rares' (CS 540) in 'The black ones they rares and they pitches', They left the spelling untouched, but Flannery corrected it to 'rears', which makes sense. In the other instance the editors made the actor 'A real swell' (CS 543). Here Flannery for obvious reasons kept the original 'A real sweal'.

With these examples I hope to have shown that Dunn 197b, Flannery O'Connor's final version of 'Judgement Day', is technically an even more satisfactory story than its three predecessors and that its characters have more depth in their relations with each other than in the published version.

The different stages in the development of the 'Judgement-Day' material have shown Flannery O'Connor on her way home artistically. The early versions show simple story telling, as do her other stories up to the publication of *Wise Blood* (1952). She worked hard for greater precision, more liveliness through dialogized passages and greater complexity through handling of point-of-view and double-edged language. We saw this in the 'An Exile in the East' version and it is true of most of her stories in *A Good Man Is Hard to Find* (1955). Also structurally her stories grow more complex, especially through her handling of time, where transitions flow seamlessly. With the final polishings of 'Judgement Day' she reached the peak of her artistic achievement, as we also know it from such stories as 'Revelation' and 'Parker's Back'. She accomplished a way of telling stories, which is unmistakably her own.

Her development as a thinker was paced in a similar way. Her stories of the forties contain messages, which they share with us on the surface. With *A Good Man Is Hard to Find* the messages can only be found on a deeper level. Though her characters are concrete, they become 'everyman', their particular experiences gain universal validity. The 'Getting Home' version clearly shows the lines along which O'Connor was thinking: she wanted the story to be more clearly Christian with an unmistakable message about the metaphysical dimension of man's life. True enough, she cut those passages again in the final version, where direct references are minimized, but they are there at the core of 'Judgement Day' as they are in the other stories, though disguised under grotesque appearances. With examples taken from her own experience in the South O'Connor shows man's situation in life, almost always against his wish 'on his way home', that is on the way back to his maker, as the author was when she finished the final version of the 'Judgement-Day' story. This material epitomizes the different phases in O'Connor's development from first promises in 'The Geranium' to final perfection in 'Judgement Day', both as artist and as thinker; it 'marks the distance she has traveled' (HB 559).

Chapter 3

Translucency in O'Connor's Settings

Place can *be transparent, or translucent: not people.*
EUDORA WELTY[1]

Striking settings – the Grand Canyon – and breathtaking views – the glory of a sunrise or the peace of a sunset – in nature as well as in art often create an unforgettable experience. Flannery O'Connor, herself an accomplished painter and cartoonist, says in her essay 'Writing Short Stories' 'a good many fiction writers … paint, not because they're good at painting, but because it helps their writing. It forces them to look at things'.[2] She was fully aware of the importance of creating in her fiction a general locale and a particular physical location, described in minute details, and she was convinced of the truth of the epistemological adage *nil in mente nisi prius in sensibus*.[3] I see O'Connor's settings as a special area of interest in her art, where precision is of paramount importance for a depth dimension to shine up. In the following I shall try to present a number of typical O'Connor settings as examples of focal points, where immanence and transcendence meet, where the particular becomes translucent.

In her seminal essay 'Place in Fiction' Eudora Welty insists on the importance of the description of particulars so that 'place can be seen'[4] and she argues, that 'fiction depends for its life on place'[5] also as a means of defining character. Rather surprisingly for Welty she states that place can be transparent, or translucent. What she means by this

---

1 Welty, Eudora, 'Place in Fiction' in *The Eye of the Story*, New York, Random House, 1990, p. 121.
2 O'Connor, Flannery, *Mystery and Manners*, eds Robert and Sally Fitzgerald, New York, Farrar, Straus & Giroux, 1969, 93.
3 'Nothing in the mind unless it was first in the senses'. In 'Writing Short Stories' she says that the writer must exercise 'the time and patience … required to convince *through the senses*'. (MM 91; my emphases.)
4 Welty, Eudora, op.cit. 116.
5 Ibid. 118.

translucency she defines later in her essay: 'From the dawn of man's imagination, place has enshrined the spirit; as soon as man stopped wandering and stood still and looked about him, he found god in that place; and from then on, that was where the god abided and spoke from if ever he spoke'.[6] Here Eudora Welty indicates, I think quite indisputably, the possibility of divine presence in place. In an earlier essay on 'The Reading and Writing of Short Stories' Miss Welty asked why some great stories keep spellbinding readers. It is because they are 'apocalyptic' and 'because they keep their power of *revealing* something' and with D.H. Lawrence she 'thinks the *transcending* thing is found *direct through the senses* [my emphases]'.[7]

Like Eudora Welty and D.H. Lawrence, Flannery O'Connor was convinced that the *non plus ultra* for her writing was 'translating her attentive eye into sensory detail for her fiction',[8] since 'the things we see, hear, smell, and touch affect us long before we believe anything at all' (MM 197). On the basis of this primary experience the writer creates a setting, a country, a universe that is unmistakably his own. O'Connor's multifarious settings are in the final analysis renderings of the same country which should lead the character to a recognition of his/her 'true country', as it happens to Mrs. Shortley at the moment of her death: 'her eyes like blue-painted glass, seemed to contemplate for the first time the tremendous frontiers of her true country'.[9] To O'Connor the word country 'suggests everything from the actual countryside that the novelist describes, on to and through the peculiar characteristics of his region and his nation, and on, through, and under all of these to his true country, which the writer with Christian convictions will consider to be what is eternal and absolute' (MM 27).

Already in the early days of O'Connor criticism Robert Fitzgerald[10] and Carter Martin[11] drew attention to the importance of her descrip-

---

6 Ibid. 123.

7 Welty, Eudora, 'The Reading and Writing of Short Stories' in Current-Garcia, Eugene & W.R. Patrick, eds, *What is the Short Story?*, Glenview, Ill., Scott, Foresman and Comp., 1961, 109, 111, 113.

8 Freeman, Mary Glenn, 'Flannery O'Connor and the Quality of Sight: A Standard for Writing and Reading' in *The Flannery O'Connor Bulletin*, vol. 16, 1987, 26.

9 O'Connor, Flannery, *Collected Works*, ed. Sally Fitzgerald, New York, The Library of America, 1988, 305.

10 Fitzgerald, Robert, 'The Countryside and the True Country' in Harold Bloom, ed., *Flannery O'Connor*, New York, Chelsea House Publishers, 1986, 19-30.

11 Martin, Carter W., *The True Country: Themes in the Fiction of Flannery O'Connor*, Nashville, Vanderbilt University Press, 1969.

tion of the countryside and her often violent settings. Some critics were
'overwhelmed by the lack of beauty in the landscape',[12] others described her landscapes as Edenic and her cities as hellish and evil.[13]
According to Jack Dillard Ashley 'nature, like the hostile human intruders, frequently functions as a scourge to punish O'Connor's characters and prepare them for grace'[14] and Flannery O'Connor herself stated that 'violence is strangely capable of returning my characters to
reality and preparing them to accept their moment of grace'.[15]

No matter how one views O'Connor's settings, they are not there
'for their own sake' since the writer 'selects every word for a reason,
every incident for a reason, every detail for a reason, and arranges them
in a certain time-sequence for a reason' (MM 75). For O'Connor 'the
artist penetrates the concrete world in order to find at its depths the
image of its source, the image of ultimate reality' (MM 157).

The writer, the reader – and certainly also the characters in O'Connor's fiction – have to develop what she called a 'habit of art', which is
'the way one learns to look at things, a habit of depth perception' (MM
64). The reader 'who is developing the "habit of art" must train his eyes
to the disciplined observation of detail, developing the skill of seeing
the surface while at the same time peering into the depths'.[16] As I will
show below, many of O'Connor's characters come to see and experience depth in the settings that surround and even form them, others do
not reach insight, they can only see 'nothing'. 'Short-sighted' characters
can see and understand nothing, nature 'can tell them no thing which
they wish to know because they cannot penetrate its physical presence
to the spiritual reality which it is'.[17] Flannery O'Connor was aware of
this fact and accordingly she adapted her technique to it, since 'to the
hard of hearing you shout, and for the almost-blind you draw large and
startling figures' (MM 34). She needed to find narratives, a language,
settings and characters, which could draw the reader into the depth

12 Chow, Sung Gay, '"Strange and Alien Country": An analysis of Landscape in Flannery O'Connor's *Wise Blood* and *The Violent Bear It Away*' in *The Flannery O'Connor
Bulletin*, vol. 8, 1979, 36.

13 E.g. Cleary, Michael, 'Environmental Influences in Flannery O'Connor's Fiction' in
The Flannery O'Connor Bulletin, vol. 8, 1979, 20-34.

14 Quoted in Nancy B. Sederberg, 'Flannery O'Connor's Spiritual Landscape: A Dual
Sense of Nothing' in *The Flannery O'Connor Bulletin*, vol. 12, 1983, 22.

15 Quoted ibid. 23.

16 Freeman, Mary Glenn, op.cit. 30.

17 Nancy B. Sederberg, op.cit. 21.

dimension of the universe. Flannery O'Connor used among others typological narratives from the Old and the New Testament, in which flashes of divine redemptive power are revealed. In the Old Testament she found theophanies, which are characterized by clearly described settings in which Yahweh makes himself known. The most striking ones are Yahweh's revelations to Moses in the burning bush episode and on Mount Sinai where Yahweh revealed himself in the cloud. In the Old Testament the typical elements in Yahweh's theophanies are summed up as follows: 'These words the Lord spoke to all your assembly at the mountain out of the midst of the fire, the cloud, and the thick darkness, with a loud voice' (Deut 5:22). The Old Testament theophanies prefigure similar New Testament revelations of the divine nature of Jesus. Most prominent is the theophany which occurred in the transfiguration of Jesus (Mt 17:1-9). It is important for our understanding of O'Connor's use of these theophanies to notice the ingredients in these happenings. There is the setting on an elevation or a mountain, there is the fire, there is the cloud, there is the bright light and there is a voice from the cloud.

Another New Testament concept used in connection with divine revelation is called 'epiphany', when the divine nature of Jesus shines up e.g. for the shepherds and the wise men who recognize God in the poor child Jesus (Mt 2:9-11). James Joyce took over and changed the concept of epiphany as an important element in his understanding of art. For him it designated the moment when something normal becomes translucent. In his early novel fragment *Stephen Hero* Stephen defines the concept as follows: 'By an epiphany he meant a *sudden* [my emphasis] spiritual manifestation, whether in the vulgarity of speech or of gesture or in a memorable phase of the mind itself. He believed that it was for the man of letters to record these epiphanies with extreme care, seeing that they themselves are the most delicate and evanescent of moments'.[18] In the pre-Joycean biblical sense the revealing power lies with the spiritual godhead. Here the subject is more passive, and it is in this sense that O'Connor lets her characters experience epiphanies. As Carol Shloss observed, O'Connor 'tended to emphasize a divine movement–human response pattern, whereby people are no longer agents of epiphany through the movements of their minds but the recipients of

---

18 Joyce, James, *Stephen Hero*, ed. by Theodore Spencer, New York, New Directions Paperback, 1963, 211.

some great and even unsought knowledge'.[19] Settings and especially landscapes seemed to O'Connor particularly conducive to 'showing grace working through nature' (MM 197).[20] Michael Cleary described O'Connor's depiction of the country as 'the touchstone' which 'is often the locale for a religious epiphany which O'Connor has termed a moment of grace'.[21]

In the following I shall first analyze three settings from O'Connor's fiction to show how she uses them as 'the concrete dramatization of what the writer has perceived in depth'.[22] After that I shall highlight three images of translucency, which play a particularly prominent role in her fiction: the peacock's tail, the tree line and the sun.

In the opening paragraph of her first novel *Wise Blood* Hazel Motes, the main character, looking out of the train window observes the following scene: 'The train was racing through tree tops that fell away at intervals and showed the sun standing, very red, on the edge of the farthest woods. Nearer, the plowed fields curved and faded and the few hogs nosing in the furrows looked like large spotted stones' (CW 3). From his vantage point Haze observes – impressionistically – the foreground as racing treetops, the middle ground as spotted stones and the far horizon as the red sun on the edge of the woods. A detailed description of a three-dimensional picture of a sunset with the red sun touching the tree line in the distance as typical elements. The opening of chapter 3 of the novel depicts a dark evening sky above the township of Taulkinham: 'The black sky was underpinned with long silver streaks that looked like scaffolding and depth on depth behind it were thousands of stars that all seemed to be moving very slowly as if they were about some vast construction work that involved the whole order of the universe and would take all time to complete. No one was paying any attention to the sky' (CW 19). O'Connor's laconically short last sentence stands in striking contrast to the long clause preceding it with

19 Shloss, Carol, 'Epiphany' in Bloom, Harold, ed., *Flannery O'Connor*, New York, Chelsea House Publishers, 1986, 69.

20 Ralph C. Wood has argued that for O'Connor as a Catholic writer 'nature and grace are inseparably united' since she sees 'the whole created order through the clarifying and transforming lens of the Incarnation'. Review of Edward Kessler, *Flannery O'Connor and the Language of Apocalypse* (Princeton, Princeton University Press, 1986) in *The Flannery O'Connor Bulletin*, vol. 15, 1986, 89.

21 'Environmental Influences in Flannery O'Connor's Fiction' in *The Flannery O'Connor Bulletin*, vol. 8, 1979, p. 34.

22 Freeman, Mary Glenn, op.cit. 26.

its well-drawn picture of the universe as a construction site. But as Haze observes, none of the people of the town pursuing their shopping needs are aware of the grandeur arching above them: they are blind to its beauty. Mary Glenn Freeman has drawn attention to the fact that O'Connor in the revision process of *Wise Blood* took heed of her literary adviser Caroline Gordon's comment that she could not 'see' Haze in the scene in chapter 13 after the patrolman had pushed Motes' car over the embankment.[23] O'Connor's change for the published version proves her attempt to add greater depth to the scene and show its effect upon Haze. After the original sentence: 'Haze stood for a few minutes looking over at the scene', where 'the scene' is not particularized in any way, she added: 'His face seemed to reflect the entire distance across the clearing, the entire distance that extended from his eyes to the blank gray sky that went on, depth after depth, into space' (CW 118). This is the moment that brings about his self-recognition.

The title of the story 'A Circle in the Fire' harks back to the Old Testament Book of Daniel, where three Jews were thrown into King Nebuchadnezzar's 'burning fiery furnace', because they refused to worship his gods. They stayed unharmed 'in the midst of the fire' because an angel looking 'like a son of the gods' had cleared a circle in the fire for them, which led to Nebuchadnezzar's acceptance of their God, Yahweh (Dan 3:11-28). Flannery O'Connor ends her story on a note of no harm to the three 'hungry' city boys Powell Boyd, Garfield Smith and W.T. Harper who had intruded upon Mrs. Cope, a typically possessive O'Connor farmer. The vigilant observer of the power game between the boys and Mrs. Cope is the child who 'could see the column of smoke rising and widening unchecked inside the granite line of trees. She stood taut, listening, and could just catch in the distance a few wild high shrieks of joy as if the prophets were dancing in the fiery furnace, in the circle the angel had cleared for them' (CW 251). The 'granite line of trees' links the ending of the story to its very beginning: 'Sometimes the last line of trees was a solid gray blue wall a little darker than the sky but this afternoon it was almost black and behind it the sky was a livid glaring white' (CW 232). The angry and threatening atmosphere created by the trees and the sky is echoed in Mrs. Cope's state of mind: she 'worked at the weeds and nut grass as if they were an evil sent directly by the devil to destroy the place' (CW 232). Mrs. Cope paranoia-

---

23 Ibid. 32.

cally feels under constant threat, be it from the weeds, from a hurricane, from fire – or from the three boys. Her woods are described as a 'fortress line of trees [which] was a hard granite blue' (CW 247). Though they seem strong the child experiences the sky behind them as more powerful: 'The child thought the blank sky looked as if it were pushing against the fortress wall, trying to break through' (CW 232). The sun actually breaks through, and Mrs. Cope is aware of the glory of the sunset. She tells the child: "'Get up and look at the sunset, it's gorgeous. You ought to get up and look at it."' The child, who *can* see, reminds Mrs. Cope of her blind fixation: "'It looks like a fire. You better get up and smell around and see if the woods ain't on fire"' (CW 233). A few minutes later they are all 'looking at the sun which was going down in front of them, almost on top of the tree line. It was swollen and flame-colored and hung in a net of ragged cloud as if it might burn through any second and fall into the woods' (CW 241). In spite of the spectacularity of the sight Mrs. Cope does not come to recognize its deep meaning. A little later when 'the sun burned so fast that it seemed to be trying to set everything in sight on fire' (CW 241) Mrs. Cope is still unable to see the true significance of the sun: it does not actually set anything on fire – that is the only thing she *can* sense. The text underlines that 'it seemed' or it looked 'as if', thus indicating that the importance of the fire of the sun is a different one. The next morning the power of the rising sun is tuned down, it is now only 'a white hole' of 'pale gold' 'like an opening for the wind [the spirit] to escape through' (CW 247). The moment of new insight [grace] has passed unrecognized by Mrs Cope, and now the destructive fire ignited by the boys takes its toll and shows its effect upon her as 'the face of the new misery' (CW 250).

In 'A View of the Woods' their radically different view on the woods leads to the deaths of Mary and her grandfather, Mr. Fortune. Though Mr. Fortune, who boasts of being a man of progress and who wants a future town named after him, is led to a moment where insight was possible, he does not want to see the signs that the setting signals, nor does he want to listen to Mary's warnings. Right from the beginning of the story O'Connor underlines the importance of the woods by personifying them: 'The red corrugated lake ... was bordered on the other side by a black line of woods which appeared at both ends of the view to *walk across the water* [my emphases] and continue along the edge of the fields' (CW 525). Mary 'stared across the lot ... to the sullen line of black pine woods fringed on top with green. Behind that line was a narrow gray-blue line of more distant woods and beyond that nothing but the sky, entirely blank except for one or two threadbare clouds. She looked into this scene as if it were a person' (CW 537).[24] Apart from the personification we have recognizable elements of a significant setting: 'the line of woods', 'the line of more distant woods', 'nothing but the sky' and 'threadbare clouds'. Their significance, however, is beyond Mr. Fortune: 'The old man looked across the road to assure himself again that there was *nothing* [my emphasis] over there to see' (CW 537). Later, in the afternoon, Mr. Fortune is alone in his room and he tries to understand what it is that Mary sees in the woods:

'The third time he got up to look at the woods, it was almost six o'clock and the gaunt trunks appeared to be raised in a pool of red light that gushed from the almost hidden sun setting behind them. The old man stared for some time, *as if for a prolonged instant he were caught up out of the rattle of everything that led to the future and were held there in the midst of an uncomfortable mystery that he had not apprehended before* [my emphases]. He saw it, in his hallucination, as if someone were wounded behind the woods and the trees were bathed in blood' (CW 538).

Mr. Fortune had for an instant the experience of being in the presence of mystery, triggered by his view of the woods, but to him it is a hallucination and when he closes his eyes, his blindness of perception is punished with the sight of 'hellish red trunks'. The next morning the sky 'was an unpleasant gray and the sun had not troubled to come out' (CW 540). As in 'The Circle in the Fire' this is a sign that the moment of insight has passed unrecognized. Again the trees are personified to witness Mr. Fortune's 'inadvertent' killing of Mary and his own fatal heart attack. 'Then he fell on his back ... On both sides of him he saw that the gaunt trees had thickened into mysterious dark files that were marching across the water and away into the distance' (CW 546). The 'mysterious dark files' march 'away into the distance' leaving the dying Mr. Fortune behind, isolated and desperate. At this point I think it is interesting to quote part of the interpretive discussion about 'A View of the Woods' that O'Connor had with her friend 'A', who had thought of Mary's father, Mr. Pitt, as a Christ symbol. O'Connor answered in her

---

24 In her article on 'Flannery O'Connor's Spiritual Landscape' Nancy B. Sederberg drew attention to the prominent element of personification in O'Connor's fiction: 'the natural landscape becomes personified as an active force which either presages or actually perpetrates the characters' confrontations with their moment of grace. The most pervasive image O'Connor employs is the penetration of some natural barrier, usually a tree line, by an agent such as a swollen red sun, or even a bull/bullet, creating a gaping bloody wound or hole' (op. cit. 21).

letter of December 28, 1956: 'I had that role cut out for the woods. ... the woods, if anything, are the Christ symbol. They walk across the water, they are bathed in a red light, and they in the end escape the old man's vision and march off over the hills. ... Part of the tension of the story is created by Mary Fortune and the old man being images of each other but opposite in the end. One is saved and the other is dammed [sic]' (HB 189-90).

While Mrs. Cope and Mr. Fortune do not understand the signs of transcendence in nature, other characters do so and experience moments of deep insight or 'grace'. In some of O'Connor's stories the peacock is an integral part of the setting and the glory of its ocellated tail is often a sign that a character is being offered a moment of insight. The priest in 'The Displaced Person' experiences such a moment: 'The cock ... raised his tail and spread it with a shimmering timbrous noise. Tiers of small pregnant suns floated in a green-gold haze over his head. The priest stood transfixed, his jaw slack ... "Christ will come like that!" he said in a loud gay voice and wiped his hand over his mouth and stood there, gaping'[25] (CW 317). The use of the words 'transfixed' and 'gaping' indicates that the priest is 'beyond' himself at this moment of divine presence in nature. O'Connor's description of the priest here is similar to that of fourteen-year-old Parker in 'Parker's Back' at his first moment of transformation in the presence of the tattooed man at the fair (CW 658).

The other two prominent examples of translucency, the tree line and the sun, are often closely interconnected. In my comments on 'A Circle in the Fire' and on 'A View of the Woods' I have already mentioned the importance of the interaction between the tree line and the sun as an intersection between the immanent setting and its transcendent meaning. Douglas Powers has drawn attention to the importance of tree lines in O'Connor's fiction. He painted twenty pictures with O'Connor tree lines[26] and gave the following explanation of his enthusiasm for them: 'In time I came to think of the treelines [sic] in O'Connor's fiction as zones of tension, a phrase used to describe the treelines of nature found

---

25 The word 'transfixed' is used in connection with the crucifixion of Jesus (Jn 19:34, 37).

26 They were exhibited in the Martha J. Dillard Mary Vinson Memorial Library, Blackbridge Hall, during the 'Habit of Art' Conference held between April 13 and 16, 1994 at Georgia College, Milledgeville, Ga. Six of them had previously been reproduced in vol. 20, 1991 of *The Flannery O'Connor Bulletin*, 55-60.

in certain mountain ranges. ... conditions above which no trees can grow. Flora has changed as elevation has increased, but the final tree-line is abrupt'.[27] Douglas Powers' information that the final change between trees and naked rock in nature is 'abrupt' is interesting, because that is precisely what characterizes O'Connor's tree lines: they are indicative of a 'sudden' break-through of the transcendent in the immanent, which may lead to a character's flash of insight, much in the same way as an 'epiphany' is a sudden spiritual manifestation. The morning light has such an effect upon Parker in 'Parker's Back': 'The sky had lightened slightly and there were two or three streaks of yellow floating above the horizon. Then as he stood there, a tree of light burst over the skyline. Parker fell back against the door as if he had been pinned there by a lance' (CW 673). In *The True Country* Carter Martin had already argued that 'the sun represents ... the light of God, to be accepted but not forced'.[28] Nancy Sederberg summarizes that 'the sun always emerges as a personification of God's patient power against the puny projections of man's pride'.[29]

In O'Connor's second novel *The Violent Bear It Away* the sun plays an important part in helping the main character, young Tarwater, along in his final stages towards acceptance of his calling as a prophet. In the penultimate chapter he says 'he would have liked for [the sun] to get out of the sky altogether or to be veiled in a cloud' (CW 465) since he feels its impact so strongly. 'The sun, from being only a large ball of glare, was becoming distinct like a large pearl, as if sun and moon had fused in a brilliant marriage' (CW 465). In the last chapter, when 'the sun, red and mammoth, was about to touch the treeline [*sic*]' (CW 474), he finally gives in and accepts his calling and the command: 'GO WARN THE CHILDREN OF GOD OF THE TERRIBLE SPEED OF MERCY' (CW 478).

The most direct description of a 'vision' triggered by the setting is to be found in the final section of 'The Revelation', where the protagonist [Mrs. Turpin] 'bent her head slowly and gazed, as if through the very heart of mystery, down into the pig parlor at the hogs. ... Until the sun slipped finally behind the tree line, Mrs. Turpin remained there with her gaze bent to them as if she were absorbing some abysmal life-

---

27 Powers, Douglas, 'Flannery O'Connor's Treelines' in *The Flannery O'Connor Bulletin*, vol. 20, 1991, 54. The tree line is also called 'timber line'.
28 Op. cit. 183.
29 Op. cit. 28.

giving knowledge. At last she lifted her head. There was only a purple streak in the sky, cutting through a field of crimson, ... A visionary light settled in her eyes. She saw the streak as a vast swinging bridge[30] extending upward from the earth through a field of living fire. Upon it a vast horde of souls were rumbling toward heaven. ... In a moment the vision faded but she remained where she was, immobile. ... In the woods around her the invisible cricket choruses had struck up, but what she heard were the voices of the souls climbing upward into the starry field and shouting hallelujah' (CW 653-54).

Though the explicitness of this example is atypical I want to conclude with this instance of O'Connor's incarnational art, where the setting for a character who clearly belongs to the group described by O'Connor as 'almost blind' and 'hard of hearing' in an instant of insight – grace – becomes both translucent and 'personant'.

---

30 The image is reminiscent of the rainbow as Yahweh's sign of contract with Noah (Gen 9:13) and of Jacob's ladder (Gen 28:12).

Chapter 4

'Parker's Back' and O'Connor's Use of Teilhardian Imagery

Flannery O'Connor herself leads up to an important source of the tattooing in 'Parker's Back'. In a letter to 'A', dated July 17, 1964, she writes: 'I found out about tattooing from a book ... called *Memoirs of a Tattooist*. The old man that wrote it took tattooing as a high art and a great profession. No nonsense. Picture of his wife in it – very demure Victorian lady in off-shoulder gown. Everything you can see except her face and hands is tattooed. Looks like fabric. *He Did It*'.[1]

A quick look at the book O'Connor mentions here proves that she has taken many details from this source and worked them into 'Parker's Back'. 'The old man' was George Burchett, 'The King of Tattooists', who died on Good Friday, 1953, eighty-one years old. He did not actually 'write' the book, but Peter Leighton, a friend of his, edited and compiled it from the tattooist's notes, diaries, and letters.[2] George Burchett certainly took his profession seriously. His editor describes him as a great dedicated artist. Burchett collapsed and died in the process of preparing for an appointment to whiten a red nose. 'Thus the last action of the cheerful, knowledgeable and skilful "King of Tattooists" was directed towards the ancient and intimate craft of which he was a great master' (Memoirs, 5). This may be one of the reasons why Flannery O'Connor refers to the tattooists in 'Parker's Back' only in one instance as 'tattooist' (CS 524) and in twenty-five cases as 'artist'.

---

1 Fitzgerald, Sally, ed., *The Habit of Being*, New York, 1979, 593-594.
2 Burchett, George, *Memoirs of a Tattooist*, edited by Peter Leighton, Oldbourne, London, 1958; hereafter abbreviated Memoirs in the text. The publication date coincides with the fact that Flannery O'Connor started working on 'Parker's Back' in the fall of 1960. Cf. her two remarks to 'A' about it: 'I am working on that story I told you about and having the best time I have had in a spell of working. If I can work it out, I'll have something here'. (December 24, 1960, HB 424) And on January 21, 1961, she wrote: '"Parker's Back" is not coming along too well. It is too funny to be serious as it ought. I have a lot of trouble with getting the right tone'. (HB 427)

The picture of Burchett's wife is found facing p. 208. Burchett thought of many of the tattoos he had put on his wife as masterpieces and he was annoyed when she later took to long-sleeved dresses closed tight at the neck: 'I thought it was a real shame – and rather a waste of time having done all these beautiful pictures which she now so determinedly concealed' (Memoirs, 220). In a similar way Parker is annoyed that his wife preferred him 'dressed and with his sleeves rolled down' (CS 519). Flannery O'Connor does not mention in her letter to 'A' that Burchett's wife had tattoos all over, that 'the left leg bears the reproduction of the crucifixion with two archangels flanking the cross with a carefully designed figure of Our Lord. On her right leg is a large angel with spread-out wings' (Memoirs, 219). Certainly the tattoos visible on the portrait photo of Mrs. Burchett 'look like fabric'. Fourteen-year-old Parker had admired the 'single intricate design of brilliant color' (CS 512) he saw on the man in a fair. Similarly he was dissatisfied that the effect of the tattoos he had put on his own body 'was not of one intricate arabesque of colors but something haphazard and botched' (CS 514). Parker 'did not care much what the subject (i.e., of a tattoo) was so long as it was colorful' (CS 514). In this way he resembles 'the Worst Man in the World' of whose tattooed face we see a picture in Burchett's book (Memoirs, facing p. 177) and who had no wish for special designs, as long as they gave the impression of a 'gay embroidery pattern' (Memoirs, 173).

My remarks in connection with Flannery's letter to 'A' show already that *Memoirs of a Tattooist* influenced certain details in her story. But there are many more parallels. Burchett had been in the Navy for twelve years, (Memoirs, 56) while Parker served only five (CS 513). The technique of tattooing that we find described in 'Parker's Back' is derived to a large extent – often down to word to word formulations – from Burchett. The choice of the design is entirely up to the customer: for Burchett 'the patron is an absolute "master"' (Memoirs, 64) and in the story the artist asked Parker, '"You found what you want?"' (CS 552). When the artist got to work, 'he swabbed his [Parker's] back with ethyl chloride and then began to outline the head on it with his iodine pencil' (CS 523). Burchett explains: 'After the customer has decided on the design he desires, the picture is outlined on the skin with an iodine pencil, after applying an anaesthetic, mainly ethyl chloride, which "freezes" the skin and also acts as an antiseptic' (Memoirs, 66). 'Another hour passed before he took up his electric instrument', we read in 'Parker's Back' (CS 523). Burchett was the one who invented this 'electric tattooing instrument' (Memoirs, 66). 'Parker felt no pain', (CS 523) while the artist was at work and earlier he had remarked about the time when he received his first tattoo, 'It hurt very little!' (CS 513) Burchett tells us that 'all my clients agree that tattooing is practically painless' (Memoirs, 67). 'While the normal tattooing operation is not painful ... the tattooing of such heavy marks as the inch-wide lines[3] must have caused some pain and distress' (Memoirs, 168). The artist in the story shares this concern in connection with the color blocks in the face of the Byzantine Christ:

"'You don't want all those little blocks though, just the outline and some better features."

"Just like it is," Parker said, "just like it is or nothing."

"It's your funeral," the artist said'. (CS 522)

On the second day the artist worked uninterruptedly 'hardly pausing with the electric instrument except to wipe the dripping dye off Parker's back as he went along' (CS 525). Burchett tells of the necessity for this procedure: 'During the process the area is constantly wiped because the dye tends to run out from the needles and any surplus of the coloring matter which is not injected into punctures must be swabbed away' (Memoirs, 66).

After the first day's work on Parker's final tattoo, the artist 'propped one mirror ... on a table by the wall and took a smaller mirror off the lavatory wall and put it in Parker's hands. Parker stood with his back to the one on the table and moved the other until he saw a flashing burst of color reflected from his back' (CS 523). On one occasion Burchett tells a client: '"You can have a look in the mirror now"'(Memoirs, 180). But when the picture is finished Parker does not care to look at it, a fact which, understandably, irritates the artist. 'The artist took him roughly by the arm and propelled him between the two mirrors. "Now look," he said, angry at having his work ignored' (CS 525). Concerning a customer who had had a red devil put on his back and who later felt persecuted by the devil and therefore wanted the otherwise beautiful picture to be removed, Burchett writes, 'Hell knows no fury like an artist scorned' (Memoirs, 162).

Burchett also proves to be Flannery's source for the tattoos that Parker had put on at earlier stages: 'In Japan he [Parker] had had a tat-

---

3   I.e. of the 'Zebra-design' that Burchett put all over the body of the so-called 'zebra-man'.

too of the Buddha done on his upper arm with ivory needles; in Burma, a little brown root of a man had made a peacock on each of his knees using thin pointed sticks, two feet long, amateurs had worked on him with pins and soot' (CS 523). 'The Japanese method is prodding. The ivory needle is used', Burchett tells us (Memoirs, 65). 'The Burmese … use thin pointed sticks almost two feet long' (Memoirs, 65). And finally Burchett confesses, 'As a boy I did use soot myself' (Memoirs, 68).

Burchett also reports people using the Bible for religious tattoos,[4] an idea that Parker also had considered (CS 519). In the photo facing p. 193 we see Burchett and his son Leslie devising designs for the coronation of Queen Elizabeth II, in 1953. The accompanying text runs: 'Right up to his death he had been working until late hours every day to cope with the many orders for portraits of the young Queen, many of which now permanently adorn her loyal subjects' chests, backs and arms'. Parker had 'Elizabeth II and Philip over where the stomach and the liver were respectively' (CS 514).

Also the idea of a man 'tattooed from head to foot' (CS 512) Flannery took from Burchett, where the plate facing p. 15 shows such a man. 'The world, of course, thought such people rather horrifying freaks'.[5] Concerning the artist himself Flannery tells us that he had put tattoos on his own body, even on the top of his head (CS 521). Burchett says about himself, 'I only had my longsuffering self on which to practise' (Memoirs, 172).

Many of the tattoos mentioned in 'Parker's Back' and not discussed so far are also found in Burchett's book. The most common religious motifs are, according to Burchett, a cross, the face of Mary, the crucifixion scene, angels, the devil (Memoirs, 75). The fact of a Byzantine Christ, however, I could not find in Burchett. Where did Flannery get this idea?

---

4   'A clergyman … had a picture of the Crucifixion scene tattooed on his chest with Bible texts round it'. (Memoirs, 175) 'Jim Harris, a seaman, had the whole of his back covered with lengthy quotations from the Bible'. Ibid. 162.

5   Memoirs, 163. I should like to remind the reader about the way in which Flannery saw most of her characters as freaks.

THE BYZANTINE CHRIST WITH
ALL-DEMANDING EYES

We need not here discuss the great importance of the face with 'eyes to be obeyed', (CS 527) which, according to the details in 'Parker's Back' seems to be the image of the Byzantine 'Pantocrator'. But why did Flannery O'Connor use this picture of Christ? Did she have a copy of it in front of her while writing the story?

One thing is certain: during the last month of her life, while Flannery was working on 'Parker's Back', she was fascinated by the Byzantine rite. On March 12, 1964, she wrote to Janet McKane: 'You are mighty nice to have the high Mass said for me in the Byzantine rite church' (HB 569). On April 2 she informs the same friend: 'I read my Mass prayers this morning, not Byzantine by any means but with much appreciation of what you were doing for me' (HB 572). Finally, four days later she wrote to the same addressee: 'I was interested to hear about the Byzantine Mass' (HB 572).

Did Janet McKane send Flannery a copy of the 'Pantocrator', I asked myself, or did Flannery have a book with the picture on her shelves? I ran through Flannery's books in the Flannery O'Connor Room at Georgia College, Milledgeville, and found a copy of Edward Rice's *The Church: Pictorial History*[6] with a picture on p. 38 of Christ as the all-powerful king. However, the picture here seems too small for it to have been the source of the colorful description of the 'Pantocrator' on Parker's back. I asked Mr. Gerald Becham, the always kind, helpful, and well-informed curator of the Flannery O'Connor collection, if he knew of a book of iconography in Flannery's room at Andalusia, to which access was barred. He thought there was such a book. I then asked the expert, Sally Fitzgerald, and in a letter of July 15, 1982, she writes, 'I think that the Pantocrator image came from a book that was given to her, I believe, by her anonymous correspondent. I don't think that Janet McKane sent her Byzantine images, although they did discuss the Eastern Rite Church'. For the time being, then, that must remain our tentative answer.

However, during my stay at the collection, Gerald Becham drew my attention to a 1973 issue of the *Atlanta Journal and Constitution Magazine*. I was struck with a puzzling surprise!

---

6   Farrar, Straus and Giroux, New York, 1961.

AN INSTANCE OF CROSS-FERTILIZATION?

Under the heading 'One night in a tattoo parlor' I saw in the issue of August 7[7] an interview with the second-generation Augusta tattoo artist Ted Don Inman. Among many tattoo designs there was also a head of Christ. Stimulated by this, I ran through the article and found structural similarities with 'Parker's Back'.

First we read about the available designs: 'snakes coiled about dripping daggers, hearts pierced with stilettos, majestic spread eagles … a head of Christ, bloody crucifix, horned Satans …'[8] One of Inman's female customers asked, 'I wonder if it hurts?'[9] Inman too had been in the Navy, he refers to himself as an artist, and he also tattooed himself.[10] We see Inman outline a heart with a dagger and scroll which bears the name 'Jacalyn'.[11] Inman uses the technique indicated in 'Parker's Back'. The design 'he outlines with the needle in black dye'.[12]

Asked 'Does he really tattoo people's, ah, you know, private places?' Inman answered, 'Oh, Yeah'.[13] But I was most surprised when I read Inman's report: 'And then once, I put the head of Christ on a buddy's back. I guess that's my best tattoo. He's 25-26 and he was a wild son of a bitch and I put that head of Christ on his back and it changed him over'.[14] Could anything be closer to the facts of 'Parker's Back'? Parker, after all, refers to his own age as about twenty-eight (CS 521) and his final tattoo certainly 'changed him over'.[15]

Inman also reports a barroom incident. His father had tattooed his own name 'Ted' on somebody's arm 'And one day in a bar somewhere a stranger walked up and looked at the man's arm and says "Hello, Ted". Well the fella says "My name's not Ted, that's my buddy's name" but the other fella did not believe him and they almost got into a fist fight'.[16] The parallel to Parker's package shop experience seems striking.

---

7 Pp. 18-19, 22-24, 26-27.

8 Ibid. 18. Cf. CS 512, 514, 522.

9 Ibid. 18.

10 Ibid. 19, 27.

11 Ibid. 22-23. Cf. CS 513, where Parker talks about his mother: 'She would not pay for any tattoo except her name on a heart … her name was Betty Jean'.

12 Ibid. 24. Cf. CS 512.

13 Ibid. 26. Cf. CS 514. 'On his abdomen he had a few obscenities but only because that seemed the proper place for them'.

14 Ibid. 26.

15 Cf. CS 527.

16 *Journal and Constitution Magazine*, 27. Cf. CS 526-27.

My first reaction to this was: Mr. Inman must know Flannery O'Connor's story. Fortunately, Ted Don Inman, Jr., still ran his tattoo parlor in Augusta. So I asked him 'Do you know Flannery O'Connor's stories?' 'Whose?' he said. My theory collapsed instantly. But how can it be that there is such a similarity between details in 'Parker's Back' and the Inman interview? Can it be mere accident?

I then asked Mr. Inman if his father, who died in 1971 and from whom the son had taken over the parlor and all designs, had given similar press interviews. Yes, he had given one in 1960, he thought, to the *Augusta Chronicle,* but unfortunately he did not have a copy of the article. So, in the short time I had, I rushed to the Augusta public library to read through the entire year 1960 on microfilm. But I could not find the article, probably because of my hurry.

My theory is that this article is somewhat similar to the one with Mr. Ted Inman, Jr., and that Flannery O'Connor saw this interview. After all, she started work on 'Parker's Back' in the fall of 1960. And my hope is, now that I am thousands of miles away, that somebody else might run through the *Chronicle* once again and find what I believe to be an important source for Flannery O'Connor's story 'Parker's Back'. If not, we must content ourselves with this as one of the most striking examples of coincidence.

O'CONNOR, TEILHARD DE CHARDIN AND 'PARKER'S BACK'

In his article on 'The Heterodoxy of Flannery O'Connor's Book Reviews' published in *The Flannery O'Connor Bulletin* no. 5 (Autumn 1976), Ralph C. Wood contends that Flannery O'Connor certainly did not have an 'unbounded esteem for Teilhard de Chardin's work',[17] that 'while she begins as an advocate of his scientific mysticism, she gradually withdraws her endorsement of it',[18] that she finally confesses that 'his attempt to reconcile evolution and revelation is a failure',[19] and 'that Flannery O'Connor's fiction constitutes a critique rather than a vindication of Teilhard's naturalistic faith'.[20] Ralph Wood's opinion seems to be shared

17 Op.cit. 21.
18 Ibid. 23.
19 Ibid. 25.
20 Ibid. 26.

by the editors of *The Flannery O'Connor Bulletin* in their opening note. In the following pages I shall try to prove that Wood is mistaken, adducing evidence from Flannery's manuscripts and letters and in my reading of her final story to show that 'Parker's Back' is – among other things – a poetic rendering of 'Tay-ahr's'[21] theory of evolution and convergence towards the eschatological point Omega, who is Christ.

FLANNERY O'CONNOR'S INTEREST IN TEILHARD DE CHARDIN

In O'Connor's private collection of books available in the O'Connor Collection at Georgia College we find copies of the following books directly related to O'Connor's interest in Teilhard:

Teilhard de Chardin, *The Phenomenon of Man,* Harper, NY 1959 (signed by Flannery in 1959)

Teilhard de Chardin, *The Divine Milieu,* Harper, NY 1960 (signed by Flannery in 1960)

Teilhard de Chardin, *Letters from a Traveler,* Harper, NY 1962 (signed by Flannery in 1962)

Corte, Nicolas, *Pierre Teilhard de Chardin, His Life and Spirit,* Macmillan, NY, 1960 (signed by Flannery in 1960 but otherwise containing no marks from her hand)

Rabut, Oliver, *Teilhard de Chardin, A Critical Study,* Sheed & Ward, NY, 1961 (signed by Flannery in 1961 and with several marks of acceptance from her hand)

Raven, Charles E., *Teilhard de Chardin, Scientist and Seer,* Harper, NY, 1962 (signed by Flannery in 1963 and with marks of acceptance from her hand)

Tresmontant, Claude, *Pierre Teilhard de Chardin, His Thought,* Helicon, Baltimore, 1959 (signed by Flannery in 1960 with many passages marked by her)

---

21 This is Flannery O'Connor's phonetic spelling of Teilhard's name in the manuscript of her review of *The Phenomenon of Man,* p. 1. (Flannery O'Connor Collection, Russell Library, Georgia College, Milledgeville) "'Tay-ahr" is a name which future generations will know better than we do'. Permission to quote from the unpublished manuscripts was granted by The Estate of Mary Flannery O'Connor, Robert Fitzgerald, Literary Executor.

With the exception of Raven's book, Flannery O'Connor wrote reviews of all of these books.[22] She seems to have become aware of Teilhard de Chardin only after the American publication of *The Phenomenon of Man* in 1959.[23] The earliest direct reference to Teilhard is found in her letter of May 25, 1959, to Dr. T. R. Spivey, Professor of English at Georgia State University, Atlanta:[24] 'Next month there is going to be a book out from the Helicon Press on Chardin – his thought.[25] My editor … was down here to visit me last week and I was asking him about Chardin and it turned out he knew him for about a month in New York, before he died. He said he was very impressive' (HB 334). By the end of November 1959 she still had no first-hand knowledge of Teilhard: 'I haven't read Père Teilhard yet so I don't know whether I agree with you or not on *The Phenomenon of Man*.'[26] She must have been exposed to Teilhard's own writings for the first time in December 1959 as on January 2, 1960, she wrote to 'A': 'Let me know when you get ready to read Teilhard's book and I will send it to you. It is hard to read if you don't know anything about chemistry and biology and I don't, but as you get on in it, it becomes very stimulating to the imagination.'[27] Her

---

22 *The Phenomenon of Man* and Tresmontant's book in *The* [Georgia] *Bulletin,* Feb. 20, 1960; *The Divine Milieu, The Bulletin,* Feb. 4, 1961; *Letters from a Traveler, The Southern Cross,* April 27, 1963; Corte's study, *The Bulletin,* October 15, 1960; Rabut's book, *The Bulletin,* December 23, 1961. O'Connor didn't manage to write about Raven's book. The only reference to her appreciation of this study is to be found in a letter to Janet McKane, June 30, 1963, HB 527.

23 It is surprising to see a kind of congeniality with Teilhard, the paleontologist, in the earliest document from Flannery in the O'Connor collection. Dunn 1 is a poem composed by O'Connor when she was in 10th grade at Peabody School (ca. 1940). The poem is called 'The First Book' and compares our achievements today to the first results of the human mind when a caveman of the prehistoric age wrote his imaginations 'on slides of stone and clay'. If the poem had been written by the young Teilhard it would undoubtedly have been taken as an early indication of his later preoccupation with excavating prehistoric man and placing him in the evolutionary process.

24 The reader may be interested in other Spivey letters; see especially HB 294.

25 She is referring to Tresmontant's book.

26 In a letter to Spivey, November 30, 1959, HB 361.

27 HB 368. She continues to admonish 'A': 'we better hurry on down and read it before it was [*sic*] put on the Index, which I gather will be no particular reflection on the book or Père Teilhard but merely to stifle the heresies that it may generate'. This remark proves that O'Connor was aware of Rome's critical attitude to Teilhard at this early date, but that she accepted the book and its author in spite of that. So there is no 'development of Miss O'Connor's attitude towards Teilhard' as Ralph Wood states in his article. (L.c. 23)

enthusiasm for Teilhard shines through her reviews of his books and her comments in her letters. To Father Watson she wrote, 'I have been reading Père Teilhard de Chardin's *Phenomenon of Man* and I believe that he is the great Christian prophet[28] of the century. This is a book that makes demands on the scientist and the philosopher and the theologian and the poet; of these I think the artist will accept his vision quickest'.[29] This thought found its way also into her review: 'The poet, whose sight is essentially prophetic, will at once recognize in Teilhard a kindred intelligence. Teilhard's view of evolution as the spiritualizing of matter is close to the poet's. ... *The Phenomenon of Man* is a work which should bring the scientist, the artist and the theologian closer towards that convergence which Père Teilhard saw as their luminous destiny'.[30]

O'Connor showed considerable indignation when Dr. Spivey, whom she otherwise respected, did not seem to make an effort to understand Teilhard: 'From your comments on him, I can't really believe you have read the book or if you have, it was with a very hot eye and not enough sympathy to get his vision. ... This is a scientific age and Teilhard's direction is to face it toward Christ. ... Talk about this man after you know something about him. I know you don't want it but I am going to send you a book on Teilhard's thought by a Frenchman, C. Tresmontant'.[31]

Flannery O'Connor adopted Teilhardian thinking as her own, as can be seen in a remark to 'A' about a book by Richard Chase: 'Somewhere else in there he calls the Christian view of history cyclical if I am not mistaken. It is not cyclical but *evolutionary*.[32] Can it be possible that a man with this much learning knows so little about Christianity?'[33]

The first, if indirect, reference to O'Connor's reading of *The Divine Milieu* is to be found in a letter of 15 November 1960 to 'A', who at the time was experiencing a crisis. 'Resignation to the will of God does not mean that you stop resisting evil or obstacles, it means that you leave

---

28 We know about the central position of the prophet image in her fiction. The key to an understanding of Hazel Motes, Tarwater, and Parker is their prophetic character.
29 A letter dated January 17, 1960. This extremely interesting correspondence, not included in HB, was edited by John R. May under the title 'Blue-Bleak Embers: The Letters of Flannery O'Connor and Youree Watson' in *New Orleans Review* vol. 6. no, 4. pp. 336-56. The quotation is found on p. 341.
30 Manuscript of the review, p. 3.
31 Letter of 9 April, 1960, HB 388. She had reviewed Tresmontant's book favorably alongside *The Phenomenon of Man*.
32 My emphasis.
33 Letter of 1 October, 1960, HB 411.

the outcome out of your personal considerations. It is the most concern coupled with the least concern'.[34] O'Connor must have been reading *The Divine Milieu* in November for the review, which she published on February 4, 1961. Here she makes a positive assessment of this work and its predecessor: 'The sense of expectation has largely disappeared from our religion. No writer of the last few centuries is more capable of restoring that sense to the Christian world than Teilhard, whose work is both scientific and profoundly Pauline. ... [His books] will probably have the effect of giving a new face to Christian spirituality. ... *The Phenomenon of Man* is scientific and traces the development of man through chemical, biological and reflective stages of life ... this second volume is religious and puts the first in proper focus. ... It is doubtful if any Christian of this century can be fully aware of this religion until he has reseen it in the cosmic light which Teilhard has cast upon it'.[35]

On the day when the review was published, Flannery wrote to her friend 'A': 'After reading both books. I doubt that his work will be put on the Index, though I think some of the people who latch upon his thought and distort it may cause certain propositions in it to be condemned'.[36]

Flannery O'Connor's persistent enthusiasm for Teilhard's vision of the world can be seen in her choosing one of his physical propositions and 'applying [it] to a certain situation in the Southern states and indeed in all the world'.[37] It may also be indicative of her esteem for Teilhard that in the final phase of her life his axiom should also become the title of her last collection of short stories.[38]

To several of her friends she recommended Teilhard's works and critical studies about the works. Those friends are 'A' (HB 368, 430),

---

34 HB 419. This remark is in keeping with Teilhard's description of 'passive diminishments'. Cf. HB 509.

35 Manuscript of the review. In these remarks there is no indication that 'her enthusiasm for Teilhard is somewhat tempered', as Wood suggests (L.c. 24).

36 4 February, 1961, HB 430.

37 Letter to Roslyn Barnes, 19 March, 1961. The proposition is taken from Chapter 3, 2 of *The Phenomenon of Man*. O'Connor applies the proposition in a way typical of her. 'It is a title taken in full respect and with profound and necessary irony', as Robert Fitzgerald points out in his Introduction to the posthumous edition of *Everything That Rises Must Converge*, New York 1965, XXX.

38 On May 21, 1964, Flannery wrote to her agent Elizabeth McKee: 'I forgot to tell Giroux that the title *Everything That Rises Must Converge* is all right with me if he thinks that is what it ought to be' HB 580.

Robert Fitzgerald,[39] Dr. Spivey,[40] Roslyn Barnes,[41] Alfred Corn,[42] Janet McKane,[43] and Father John McCown.[44] To McCown she recommends Teilhard as the most important Catholic non-fiction writer,[45] 'who died in 1955 and has so far escaped the Index, although a monition has been issued on him. If they are good, they are dangerous' (HB 570-71). She was fully aware of the 'danger', but this did not detract her interest nor did it affect her admiration for the scientist and believer Teilhard.[46] This fact can also be seen in her review of *Letters from a Traveler*. 'The picture these letters give is one of exile, suffering and absolute loyalty to the Church on the part of a scientist whose life's effort was an attempt to fit his knowledge of evolution into the pattern of his faith in Christ'.[47]

Teilhard's discussion of 'passive diminishments' in the second part of *The Divine Milieu* exerted a particularly strong attraction on Flannery who because of her long illness had a deep understanding of suffering. By 'passive diminishments' Teilhard 'means those afflictions that you can't get rid of and have to bear. Those that you can get rid of he be-

---

39 Robert Fitzgerald recalls that Flannery O'Connor 'had been reading' Teilhard's works 'at least since early 1961 when she recommended them to me'. (Introduction to *Everything That Rises Must Converge*, XXV)

40 HB 388; cf. my earlier remarks, pp. 82-83.

41 She wrote to Barnes, 'I finally got off *The Divine Milieu* to you'. 23 January, 1961, HB 428.

42 Letter of 30 May, 1962, HB 477. 'I might suggest that you look into some of the works of Teilhard de Chardin (*The Phenomenon of Man* et al.)' In a letter of June 16, 1962, she writes, 'If you are interested, the enclosed book [*Creative Evolution*, by Teilhard de Chardin] will give you a general line of reasoning about what I do'. HB 479-80.

43 Letter of 25 February, 1963, HB 509: 'I think he was a very great man. ... I would like to send you *The Divine Milieu* but I lent my copy to somebody who didn't return it'. Letter of 17 May, 1963, 'I like Teilhard's idea of the Mass upon the World' (HB 521). From this remark we can surmise that Flannery also knew *La Messe sur le Monde*. She also recommended Raven's study of Teilhard to her: 'I am reading another book on Teilhard – by an Episcopalian. It's real good. I'd like to lend it to you when I get through if you're interested'. (HB 527)

44 Father McCown had asked to be introduced to the work of the most important Catholic fiction writers. After having mentioned some, Flannery adds Teilhard as 'the most important non-fiction writer'. (Letter of 21 March, 1964, HB 570).

45 So it is not true that Flannery revised her positive opinion about Teilhard and his work, as Wood suggests, since she wrote this letter less than five months before her death.

46 Even Wood concedes Flannery's unchanging esteem for Teilhard, the man.

47 Quoted from the manuscript of the review.

lieves you must bend every effort *to* get rid of' (HB 509). 'The patient – he's done all he can to get rid of it and can't so he's passive and accepts it' (HB 512), as did Flannery O'Connor.

WHAT DID FLANNERY O'CONNOR BORROW FROM TEILHARD?

O'Connor certainly found Teilhard difficult reading, and, knowing her limitations, she confessed, 'I don't understand the scientific end of it or the philosophical but even when you don't know those things, the man comes through. He was alive to everything there is to be alive to and in the right way'.[48] She certainly understood the main thrust of his argument and allowed it to fertilize her imagination. In her review of *The Phenomenon of Man* she underscores the thought of evolution and convergence. It 'is a work on evolution in which human life is seen as converging towards a point which Père Teilhard calls Omega and which he identifies with Christ'.[49] Similarly, she marked the following passage in Tresmontant: 'The very great importance of Teilhard's work: it is concentrated precisely on the discovery of the direction of evolution in a positive manner'.[50]

She makes Sir Julian Huxley's appraisal of Teilhard's scientific value her own: He has affected 'a threefold synthesis – of the material and physical world with mind and spirit; of the past with the future; and of variety with unity, the many with the one and … the measure of his stature is that he so largely succeeded in the search for human significance in the evolutionary process'.[51] For Teilhard all matter has a propensity towards growing complexity and converging integration. The same movement toward complexity is characteristic also of all forms of life, and all life is characterized by a cephalization, where the self-conscious human being is a person, an organism, which has taken the step from individuality to personality. In his Preface to *The Phenomenon of Man* Teilhard uses the image of the meridian to visualize the converging process of evolution. Just as do the meridians when they approach the pole,

48 Letter to Thomas Stritch of 14 September, 1961, HB 449.
49 Manuscript of the review, p. 1.
50 Op.cit. 43.
51 Manuscript of *The Phenomenon of Man* review, pp. 1-2.

sciences, philosophy and religion necessarily converge in face of the universe. In *The Divine Milieu* Teilhard applies his findings to the Christian milieu, concentrating on the divinization of human actions and passive diminishments, the latter comprising the problem of evil, and thus describing a new form of Christian ascetic life. Flannery O'Connor sympathized with this new understanding of asceticism, which no longer 'consists so much in liberating and purifying oneself from matter – but in further spiritualizing matter'.[52] Thus 'creation is still in full gestation and the duty of the Christian is to cooperate with it'.[53]

Like Teilhard, Flannery saw 'all things as in Christ – and that not figuratively but factually. For him [as for her] Christ was and is *Le Milieu Divin*, the light and life and love of the world; and evolution, the cosmogenesis is the Christification of all things'.[54] But this eschatological optimism is not blind to the existence of evil, which tries to hinder or retard the convergence towards Omega. Teilhard, 'assuming and integrating the risks of failure', holds an 'optimism' which is 'a tragic optimism'.[55] This is a realization of the paradox of Christ's crucifixion – the impact of evil – and resurrection, the irrevocable impact of 'God above'.[56]

To sum up, I want to quote *in extenso* from the leader in the issue of *Esprit* dedicated to the memory of Flannery O'Connor: 'As did Teilhard in his scientific-philosophic findings discover "an inverse form of gravitation" – the ascent of life toward spirit and of spirit toward Omega is due to an attraction from above, namely, the divine, personal, transcendent Omega, "loving and lovable at this very moment," so does Flannery O'Connor reveal in her fictional upsidedown world Man's discovery of his awful power to embrace or reject Omega in his existentially free acceptance or free refusal to love. Like Teilhard, she firmly believed: "By virtue of the Creation, and still more, of the Incarnation, nothing here below is profane for those who know how to see."'[57]

---

52 Ibid. 2.
53 Ibid.
54 Raven, op.cit. 186 and marked by Flannery with a symbol of assent.
55 Tresmontant, op.cit. 49.
56 Parker in 'Parker's Back', CS 520.
57 Vol. 8, Winter 1964, No. 1, Scranton, Penn.

A TEILHARDIAN READING OF 'PARKER'S BACK'

It is important to remember that Flannery's work on 'Parker's Back' (PB) took place in two phases with an intermittent period of more than three years. The story is first mentioned in December 1960, when she had been reading *The Divine Milieu*.[58] In her Christmas letter to 'A' we find: 'Me, I am working on that story [PB] I told you about and having the best time I have had in a spell of working. If I can work it out, I'll have something here'.[59] However, a month later she wasn't satisfied with the work: '"Parker's Back"[60] is not coming along too well. It is too funny to be as serious as it ought'.[61] She gave up work on the story and concentrated instead on 'Everything That Rises Must Converge'.[62]

Flannery resumed work on PB again in the last three months of her life, and it thus turned out to be the last story she ever wrote. First, she composed it in her head;[63] then she scratched on it 'in longhand here at the hospital at night but that's not my idea of writing'.[64] After having expressed her intense wish to finish the story[65] she could finally send a typed copy to 'A' on 11 July with a request for comments.[66] When she sent a copy to Catharine Carver four days later, she wrote: 'I have drug another out of myself and I enclose it. I think it's much better than the last[67] but I want to know what you think' (HB 593). The urgency of the appeal for comments shows how much she was concerned to get this particular story right because it contains the epitome of O'Connor's Christian world view, which is essentially Teilhardian, I think.

---

58 See my earlier remarks on pp. 83-84.

59 24 December, 1960, HB 424.

60 This is the first time the title is actually mentioned.

61 Letter to 'A' of 21 January, 1961, HB 427.

62 On 26 March, 1961 she mentions that she had finished 'Everything That Rises Must Converge', HB 436.

63 Letter to Charlotte Gafford of 10 May, 1964, HB 576. 'I am writing me this story in my head'. The title is not mentioned here, but the story mentioned can only be PB. 'Revelation' had been finished and sent to 'A' and Catherine Carver by 6 December, 1963 (HB 552) and 'Judgement Day' – in a late draft, at least – was 'finished about the same time as "Revelation"', she wrote on 17 June, 1964, HB 585.

64 To Catherine Carver on 17 June, 1964, HB 585.

65 To Robert Giroux: 28 May, 1964 (HB 581), 9 June (HB 583) and 28 June, 1964 (HB 589).

66 HB 592. The same day she also sent a copy to Caroline Gordon Tate. (HB 593)

67 She had sent 'Judgement Day' on 27 June, 1964 and asked for comments. (HB 588)

Caroline Gordon Tate and 'A' had already reacted six days after Flannery had sent the story to them. On 17 July, 1964 she informed 'A' about a telegram from Caroline 'saying some mechanical details would follow but *she thought it unique*,[68] that I had succeeded in dramatizing a heresy' (HB 593). 'A' must have commented on the barroom scene as Flannery wrote 'I enclose a better barroom scene'.[69] 'A' had also perceived, as she thought, a heresy in the story, but, as Flannery's final remark on the story shows, an entirely different one: 'No Caroline didn't mean the tattoos were the heresy. Sarah Ruth was the heretic – the notion that you can worship in pure spirit'.[70]

Why was 'A''s reading wrong? 'A' had apparently expressed the traditional attitude to tattooing as something despicable and seen Sarah Ruth as the good orthodox Christian who looks down upon tattoos as 'vanity of vanities',[71] who at the first touch of Parker's tattooed hand dropped it 'as if she had accidentally grasped a poisonous snake' (PB 512), who preferred to be 'married in the Country Ordinary's office because she thought churches were idolatrous',[72] and who consequently screamed, '"Idolatry! Idolatry! Enflaming yourself with idols under every green tree! I can put up with lies and vanity but I don't want an idolater in this house"'[73] on seeing the image of the Byzantine Christ on Parker's back.

Sarah Ruth's heresy of denying the holiness of the physical world of the senses can also be seen in such small facts as her lack of interest in sexuality: 'She would shut her eyes tight and turn her back as well. Except in total darkness, she preferred Parker dressed and with his sleeves rolled down'.[74] She showed no interest in delicious food, since she was 'no cook' and 'just threw food in the pot and let it boil' (PB 519), an activity which results in Parker's losing 'flesh'. Most important, however,

---

68 My emphases.
69 HB 593. Maybe she is here referring to the fact that in one of the late manuscript fragments of the story (Dunn 191a) she gave names to the barroom characters, but later deleted them.
70 Letter to 'A' of 25 July, 1964. (HB 594)
71 PB 515, 518, taken from Ecclesiastes 1:2.
72 PB 518. O'Connor had intensified this sentence by changing it from the original 'marriage in Churches idolatrous' to the final version. (Dunn 190d, p. 7 and 191a. p. 11 in the O'Connor Collection, Georgia College, Milledgeville.)
73 PB 529. 'Lies' refers to his false statements about the woman he worked for (PB 511), 'vanity' to his tattoos.
74 PB 519. O'Connor's typically ironic tone is obvious.

she denies the physical concreteness of God, once and for all manifest-
ed to the world in the incarnation of Christ, when she says to Parker
about God, 'He don't *look*. He's a spirit. No man shall see his face'.[75]

The names that Flannery chose certainly point in the same direction:
Sarah, which means 'princess', laughed at the three men physically rep-
resenting Yahweh at Mamre. (Cf. Genesis 18:12) However, she became
pregnant with Isaac with whom Yahweh established 'a Covenant in
perpetuity' (Genesis 17:19). In the same way Ruth ('friendship'), who is
a heathen from Moab (Ruth 1:4), gave birth to Boaz's son Obed, which
means 'servant' (of Yahweh)[76] who 'was the father of David's father,
Jesse' (Ruth 4:17). Flannery's Sarah Ruth is also pregnant and thus
comes to represent all mankind, as do her Old Testament namesakes.

Sarah Ruth's aberrant spirituality is further stressed by Flannery's deliberate choice of her family name, which she reveals in the most intimate scene of the story, after Parker had identified himself as 'Obadiah
(Obadiah 1) Elihue' (1 Samuel 1:1), which means 'servant of Yahweh –
Whose God is He'. In the early drafts Sarah Ruth's name was 'Flow-
ers'.[77] In a late fragment[78] Flannery changed it to the final 'Cates' (PB
517). I take this to be an abbreviation for the Medieval groups of
'Cathari' – the clean ones – whose strict dualism forbade them to believe that Christ had really become man. The body was regarded as
sinful, and their strict asceticism denied them all physical joy.

It was this heresy that Caroline Tate had recognized rightly in the
story[79] and which Flannery made concrete in her description of Sarah
Ruth's face: 'The skin on her face was thin and drawn as tight as the
skin on an onion and her eyes were gray and sharp like the points of
two icepicks' (PB 510). No wonder that at his first meeting with Sarah
Ruth, Parker, having spent his life and his money embellishing his body
and having jerked out of his mother's grasp when she had dragged him
to a church (PB 513), said, 'I don't want nothing to do with this one'
(PB 512). Nevertheless, 'he stayed as if she had him conjured' (PB 510).
It was only after his 'accident' with the tractor and after he had seen the
'Byzantine Christ with all-demanding eyes' (PB 522) that 'he longed

---

75 PB 529. A direct quotation of Yahweh's advice to Moses in Exodus 33:20.
76 Ruth 4:17. The name is the same as the first part in Obadiah!
77 Dunn 190b, p. 6; 190d, p. 6.
78 Dunn 191a, p. 10.
79 See above note 70.

miserably for Sarah Ruth. Her sharp tongue and icepick eyes were the only comfort he could bring to mind. He decided he was losing it. Her eyes appeared soft and dilatory compared with the eyes in the book, for even though he could not summon up the exact look of those eyes, he could still feel their penetration. He felt as though, under their gaze, he was transparent as the wing of a fly' (PB 524). How is this turnabout, this tragic irony, possible, as Sarah Ruth on his return thrashes him out of his own house? In the answer to this question I suggest lies the key to an understanding of Parker and to the entire story.

Parker had his first initiation – or call to vocation – when he saw the tattooed man at a fair: 'He was heavy and earnest, as ordinary as a loaf of bread'.[80] This is the first time he came to realize 'that there was anything out of the ordinary about the fact that he existed' (PB 513). A particular unease settled in him: he obeyed his instinct 'in rapture when his spirit had lifted at the sight of the tattooed man at the fair' (PB 527). Ever since that time, his life had had the sole aim of having his body adorned with tattoos, seeking satisfaction of the senses by having girls (PB 511), drinking beer and getting into fights (PB 513). Only his eyes seemed to suggest the destination of his vocation: In the navy 'his eyes, which were the same pale slate-color as the ocean ... reflected the immense spaces around him as if they were a microcosm of the mysterious sea'.[81]

Then occurs his first meeting with his self-righteous future wife, who 'did not approve of automobiles.[82] In addition to her other bad qualities,[83] she was forever sniffing up sin. She did not smoke or dip, drink whiskey, use bad language or paint her face' (PB 510). Parker is given another shock of awareness: Her 'terrible bristly claw slammed the side of his face and ... Parker's vision was so blurred that for an instant he thought he had been attacked by some creature from above, a giant

---

80 PB 513. The 'loaf of bread' is a first hint at the Christ-figure Parker is to become later.

81 PB 514. The eyes as microcosmic mirror of the macrocosmos is a typically Teilhardian image.

82 In an interview with Betsy Lockeridge, the carbon copy of which is in the O'Connor collection, Flannery confessed about herself: 'It's more to my taste to hear cows and chickens than carhorns and trucks' (p. 2).

83 Technically this is Parker's point of view, but in the ironic turn of the entire sentence, the author's attitude to Sarah Ruth shines through.

hawk-eyed angel wielding a hoary weapon. As his sight cleared, he saw before him a tall raw-boned girl with a broom'.[84]

Here two entirely different world-views meet, and the clash is further emphasized by Parker's repeated sexual hints: '"You ought to see the ones you can't see"' (PB 512). Inspired, Parker said, '"I'd be saved enough if you was to kiss me."'[85] And when before their marriage Parker suggested that they lie down in the back of the truck and he reached for her, 'she thrust him away with such force that the door of the truck came off and he found himself flat on his back on the ground'.[86] Parker in all this obviously represents the flesh, which in the eyes of Sarah Ruth is sinful and despicable.

Parker's tattoos and the order in which he has them put on his body are, I think, a key to a Teilhardian reading of the story. Parker has picked them up all over the world (PB 514), and in his employer's eyes he is 'a walking panner-rammer' (PB 519). At one point in the story Parker sums up: 'He had stopped having lifeless ones like anchors and crossed rifles. He had a tiger and a panther on each shoulder, a cobra coiled about a torch on his chest, hawks on his thighs, Elizabeth II and Philip over where his stomach and liver were respectively' (PB 514). Here we have precisely the same grouping that we find in Teilhard's *The Phenomenon of Man*. In the first part Teilhard deals with the universe of lifeless things, represented in the story by anchors and crossed rifles. The spiritual energy that is inherent in matter converges towards life. Therefore, the second part of the book treats the origin of life and its

---

84 PB 511-12. Parker was to feel the broom thrashing on his shoulders in his final meeting with Sarah Ruth (PB 529). As for the strong girl, see the main character in Carson McCullers'/Edward Albee's novel/play *The Ballad of the Sad Café*, which Flannery was interested in seeing in its theater version. She intensely disliked McCullers' work. (Letter to Janet McKane of 28 November, 1963, HB 550). In an early version (Dunn 190d) Parker's vision is of something much more supernatural: 'He saw the fierce shimmering figure against a background of pure gold its feet seeming not quite to touch the ground and its hand gripping upon a fantastic weapon. ... As he spoke his vision had cleared and he saw that her feet rested solidly on the ground and that the background gold was a hill of bitterweed beyond the field behind her and that it was a broom she had hit him with' (pp. 3-4). In the final version Flannery turned this down considerably so as to delete these positive epithets from Sarah Ruth and to stress the importance of Parker's later vision.

85 PB 518. Flannery wanted this more obviously sexual hint as she preferred it to the earlier 'if you was to hold my hand'. (Dunn 190d, p. 6)

86 PB 518. In the tractor 'accident' he also landed on his back.

different forms, in the story represented by tiger, panther, cobra, hawks. Life converges towards the consciousness of the noosphere: *homo sapiens* arises, which is the third part of Teilhard's book and which in the story is represented by Elizabeth II and Philip. The fourth part of the book deals with the continuation of life and the convergence of the personal sphere of life towards the point Omega, who is Christ; but I shall return to this part in a moment.

'Parker would be satisfied with each tattoo about a month.[87] ... A huge dissatisfaction would come over him and he would go off and find another tattooist and have another space filled up' (PB 514). This dissatisfaction indicates the inner energy that leads to a new step in the evolutionary process. The energy is irresistible, both in Teilhard's analysis of the universe and in Parker's search for new images. 'As the space on the front of him for tattoos decreased, his dissatisfaction grew and became general. ... His dissatisfaction, from being chronic and latent, had suddenly become acute and raged in him. It was as if the panther and the lion and the serpents and eagles and the hawks had penetrated his skin and lived inside him in a raging warfare'.[88] Parker was no longer only the bearer of these images; they came alive and possessed him. He had to have a new tattoo – and on his back (PB 519). 'A dim half-formed *inspiration*[89] began to work in his mind. He visualized having a tattoo put there that Sarah Ruth would not be able to resist – a religious subject' (PB 519). He becomes so preoccupied with the thought that he feels persecuted.[90] 'But as urgent as it might be for him to get a tattoo, it was just as urgent that he get exactly the right one to bring Sarah Ruth to heel'.[91] 'His eyes took on a hollow preoccupied expression'.[92] His longing to do something for Sarah Ruth grows; he wants to save her from her misapprehensions, out of love, 'to please her' (PB 527).

Into this longing breaks Parker's second vocation: As he was baling hay with the old tractor spiraling towards the one enormous old tree in

---

87 An indication of the different ages in the history of the earth and life on it.

88 PB 514, cf. Romans 8:22: 'From the beginning till now the entire creation, as we know, has been groaning in one great act of giving birth'.

89 My emphasis; cf. note 85.

90 A paranoia which had sent his granddaddy to a mental hospital. (PB 520)

91 PB 520, I.e. to a more humane form of religion.

92 PB 520. Cf. Tarwater's eyes at the end of *The Violent Bear It Away* and the concentration on Hazel's eyes in the final paragraph of *Wise Blood*.

the middle of the field, 'All at once he saw the tree reaching out to grasp him.[93] A ferocious thud propelled him into the air, and he heard himself yelling in an unbelievably loud voice, "GOD ABOVE!"'[94] Parker landed on his back, saw his shoes 'quickly being eaten by the fire. ... He was not in them. He could feel the hot breath of the burning tree on his face' (PB 520). The ingredients of this episode are clearly reminiscent of the burning bush episode[95] in which Yahweh revealed himself to Moses, who was ordered to take off his shoes for the place on which he stood was holy ground. The effect of this vision is a change in his life. 'He scrambled backwards, still sitting, his eyes cavernous, and if he had known how to cross himself he would have done it' (PB 520). Parker knew 'that there had been a great change in his life, a leap forward into a worse unknown, and that there was nothing he could do about it' (PB 521).

The immediate result is that Parker rushed – still barefooted – to the tattooist and demanded a tattoo of God on his back. By an irresistible and inexplicable force he was driven to the right image. 'Parker's heart began to beat faster and faster until it appeared to be roaring inside him like a great generator. He flipped the pages quickly, feeling that when he reached *the one ordained*,[96] a sign would come.[97] ... On one of the pages a pair of eyes glanced at him swiftly. Parker sped on, then stopped. His heart too appeared to cut off, there was absolute silence. It said as plainly as if silence were a language itself, GO BACK.[98] Parker returned to the picture – the haloed head of a flat stern Byzantine Christ with all-demanding eyes'.[99] This is the picture he had put on his back.

Finally the evolution of pictures on Parker's body reached its fulfillment, as the creation reached its Omega in the fourth part of Teilhard's

---

93 An image taken from Ezekiel 8:2-3 'I looked and saw something that looked like a man. Downwards from what seemed to be his loins he was fire; and upwards from his loins he seemed to shine like polished bronze. He stretched out what seemed to be a hand and took me by the hair; and the spirit lifted me into the air'.

94 Here his shout is a true invocation counterbalancing Parker's original oaths, "'God dammit! ... Jesus Christ in hell! Jesus God Almighty damm! God dammit to hell.'" (PB 511)

95 Exodus 3:2-5. The image is also used for the final vocation of Tarwater.

96 My emphases.

97 As they come to the prophets of the Old Testament.

98 This is the sign Parker had expected.

99 PB 522. As mentioned above Flannery had shown considerable interest in the Byzantine rite in the spring of 1964.

Phenomenon. This picture of the Pantocrator was put on his back, i.e., he could not see it directly, much as the fulfillment of the creation in Omega cannot yet be seen clearly.

Parker had a dreadful night after his vision, for he was still shocked when he re-experienced what had happened (PB 524). The all-demanding eyes of Christ penetrated him, and he felt transparent. Here then is the answer to the question I put earlier.[100] The eyes of Christ are 'all-demanding',[101] and compared to them Sarah Ruth's are 'soft and dilatory'.

Parker had had his vision. How did he and his surroundings react to it? Parker needed a quick 'pint of whiskey' to recover (PB 526). His drinking pals were thrilled and by force pulled up his shirt: 'Parker felt all the hands drop away instantly and his shirt fell again like a veil over the face'.[102] After moments of silence they started ridiculing him, 'Maybe he's gone and got religion' (PB 526). But Parker, like the prophet Jonah, denied his vocation: "'Not on your life.'" Like Jonah, Parker was thrown out, and the pool hall looked like 'the ship from which Jonah had been cast into the sea' (PB 527).

Finally Parker reached a state of self-knowledge:[103] 'Examining his soul, he saw it as a spider web. ... The eyes that were now forever on his back were eyes to be obeyed. He was as certain of this as he had ever been of anything. ... His dissatisfaction was gone, but he felt not quite like himself. It was as if he were himself but a stranger to himself, driving into a new country' (PB 527). This is to say, Parker had reached the knowledge that he was no longer himself but had changed into a new person who saw everything through new eyes.

He drove home, but was locked out of his own house. His wife did not recognize – or want to recognize – him. When asked about his identity, 'Parker turned his head as if he expected someone behind him[104] to give him the answer' (PB 528). The door was opened to his intimate whispering of 'Obadiah Elihue',[105] but in the same instant Parker 'felt the light pouring through him, turning his spider web soul

---

100 See my earlier remarks on this subject.

101 Used twice: p. 524 and p. 526. O'Connor's technique of concentration on the eyes of Sarah Ruth, Parker, and Christ is counterbalanced by her emphasis on the visual impression of the tattoos.

102 A reference to Leviticus 16:2: the veil in the sanctuary of the Temple.

103 At the beginning of the story 'it was himself he could not understand' (PB 510).

104 I.e., the face of Christ on his back.

into a perfect arabesque of colors, a garden of trees and birds and beasts' (PB 528). The light of Christ made him translucent and in him was all created life, here represented by trees, birds and beasts, images directly parallel to the thought of Teilhard.

But Sarah Ruth Cates – 'pure' self-righteous mankind – did not see the light, did not recognize the image of her Christ, and in her blindness threw him – Parker/Christ – out of her house. She thrashed him senseless 'and large welts had formed on the face of the tattooed Christ'(PB 529) punishing him as Jesus was punished by self-righteous Israel and scourged by Roman soldiers. Having finished her tragic execution, Sarah Ruth allowed her 'eyes [to] harden ... still more. There he was – who called himself Obadiah Elihue – leaning against the tree, crying like a baby' (PB 530). Like Jesus on the tree of the cross Parker leaned against the tree, 'Obadiah', i.e., worshiper of Yahweh, thrown out by mankind; 'Elihue', i.e., Whose God is He.

CONCLUSION

In 'Parker's Back' Flannery O'Connor has dramatized a heresy, which is the backcloth for the drama of the history of the universe from the creation to its final fulfillment in the cosmic point Omega, who is already with us in Christ. Moreover, she has dramatized Teilhard's scientific-philosophical-theological vision in a unique way. Against Sarah Ruth's bloodless denial of the flesh and heretical misunderstanding of Christian life, she places – with Teilhard – a Christian spirituality, which accepts with all its consequences that 'The Word was made flesh' (Jn 1:14). The order of the tattoos on Parker's body is the symbolic rendering of the inner life of the creation and its convergence towards Christ. However, the eschatological point Omega is not reached yet, and the entire creation is still groaning[106] under the retarding effect of evil. Only if Sarah Ruth opens her eyes to the light shining through Parker's back, i.e., only if mankind opens its eyes for Christ and freely accepts His offer, will the child of the future or the future generation, move further towards convergence in Omega.

---

105 Flannery uses the same verb here as in the intimate scene when O.E. reveals his identity to Sarah Ruth and when the name comes 'as a sign to her' (PB 517).
106 Cf. Romans 8:22.

With this story and with her other activities and passive diminishments, Flannery O'Connor contributed her part to recounting the cosmic convergence towards Christ.

Chapter 5

O'Connor's Treatment of *homo viator* in 'The Displaced Person'

Her eyes like blue-painted glass, seemed to contemplate for the first time the tremendous frontiers of her true country.

FLANNERY O'CONNOR

Displacement is more than ever an experience that a growing number of people go through. Religious, political, economic reasons have driven individuals, families and whole tribes into the diaspora of leaving their native roots and finding a new existence in a foreign environment. Identification with the place of origin, though often desirable, is no longer possible, and identification with the new place and its traditions is necessary, but not easy. More often than not this leads to a traumatic sense of displacement, of existential uprootedness.

One of the places where many ethnic groups have found a new home is North America, the continent earlier known as the land of unlimited possibilities. Large contingents of immigrants from different parts of the world have settled here, some integrating into their new environment, others trying to counterbalance their displacement by moving into ethnic neighborhoods. The resulting frictions between 'natives' and newcomers have been studied in scholarly treatises and represented in works of fiction. Among those are the works of two renowned writers of the American South, Flannery O'Connor (1925-1964) and Walker Percy (1916-1990). It is characteristic that they present 'displacement' with its physical and spiritual dimensions. Post-lapsarian man is essentially 'displaced' and 'alienated', constantly in search of his proper place and his true self. Sarah Gordon has convincingly pointed out the essential similarity between Walker Percy and Flannery O'Connor in their interest in depicting protagonists who experience themselves as alienated 'castaways' who are 'homesick'.[1] In her discussion of

---

1 Sarah Gordon, 'The News From Afar: A Note on Structure in O'Connor's Narratives', *The Flannery O'Connor Bulletin*, vol. 14 (1985), 80-87.

O'Connor's 'Poetics of Space' Christiane Beck characterizes this space as follows: 'The most conspicuous characteristic of space in this work is its pervasive hostility invariably aimed at man. The human world is shown to be an essentially homeless place, a world where children are left motherless. ... O'Connor's world is one where man is fated from his birth to live as the prey of hostile spatial powers'.[2]

In 1953/54 Flannery O'Connor wrote a short story entitled 'The Displaced Person' (first published in 1954), in which she dramatizes the meeting between a white farmer, a 'white-trash' family, a couple of black farm hands and a Polish immigrant family. The story is set in the strongly traditional American South, where the Polish family of the Guizacs arrive shortly after World War II. Mr. Guizac is the title figure of this three-part novelette, but characteristically for Flannery O'Connor the experience of displacement has much wider implications: it affects all layers in this small society, and it does not only affect them in the physical sense of the word.

The Polish immigrants carry with them the culture, habits, work ethics and religion of their home country; but otherwise they are dispossessed. Similarly, the recipient society has its social, cultural, religious and politico-economical heritage; and they are 'in possession', they are 'justified' in defending their own. The demands on both sides are tremendous.

This is what Flannery O'Connor saw and described on the surface level of 'The Displaced Person',[3] where all characters experience displacement. In the first part of the story Mrs. McIntyre, the owner of the farm, and the white-trash Shortleys are in possession of their territory, their 'place',[4] whereas the Polish refugees are seen as displaced intruders. However, at the end of this part the first crisis occurs, the Shortleys are discharged from the farm, displaced. In the second part the Guizacs are in power, Mr. Guizac has 'replaced' the Shortleys. But a new conflict arises when Mr. Guizac tries to bring over his cousin from Poland. Mrs. McIntyre cannot tolerate this violation of the rules of decorum.

---

2   Christiane Beck, 'Flannery O'Connor's Poetics of Space' in Karl-Heinz Westarp & Jan Nordby Gretlund, eds., *Realist of Distances* (Århus: Aarhus University Press, 1987), 137-38.

3   Flannery O'Connor, The Complete Stories (New York: Farrar, Straus & Giroux, 1971), 194-235.

4   'Place' occurs more than 60 times in the text alongside numerous references to 'country', 'there', and 'here'.

Part three presents the climax in which Mrs. McIntyre and the returned Mr. Shortley violently 'displace' Mr. Guizac. In turn they are displaced, as O'Connor points out in the last paragraph of the story.

Most of what we know about the Guizacs is colored by Mrs. Shortley's eyes, through which we see them. Upon their imminent arrival Mrs. Shortley stands there, the ominous 'giant wife of the countryside, come out at some sign of danger' (CS 194). Before they show up Mrs. Shortley has changed the Polish family's name into the derogatory 'Gobblehooks' and imagined the newcomers as animals. When they arrive 'The first thing that struck her as peculiar was that they looked like other people. Every time she had seen them in her imagination, the image she had got was of the three bears, walking single-file' (CS 195).[5] As far as Mrs. Shortley is concerned, they should have stayed 'over there', 'in Europe where they had not advanced as in this country' (CS 196), in a Europe which she remembers from a newsreel as a concentration camp and of which her husband only has World War I trench memories, in short a Europe 'mysterious and evil, the devil's experiment station' (CS 205). She certainly thinks that the American people have done enough for those Europeans who are

'Always fighting amongst each other. Disputing. And then get us into it. Ain't they got us into it twict already and we ain't got no more sense than to go over there and settle it for them and then they come on back over here and snoop around' (CS 206-07).

'She thought there ought to be a law against them. There was no reason they couldn't stay over there and take the places of some of the people who had been killed in their wars and butcherings' (CS 205).

Later also Mrs. McIntyre adduces defense mechanisms in saying, '"This is my place"' (CS 224) and '"I don't find myself responsible for all the extra people in the world"' (CS 226). She intends to tell Father Flynn, the priest who had brought the Guizacs to her farm, 'that *her* moral obligation was to her own people, to Mr. Shortley, who had fought in the world war for his country and not to Mr. Guizac who had merely arrived here to take advantage of whatever he could' (CS 228).

There are obvious reasons for this kind of attitude: everybody is afraid of the otherness of the newcomers, the unknown territory from which they come. And the Guizacs do behave differently in their new

---

5   In spite of their human looks Mrs. Shortley later thinks of them 'like rats with ty-phoid fleas' (CS 196), like the animal 'carcass on which the buzzard alights' (CS 197), and Mr. Guizac jumps on the tractor 'like a monkey' (CS 202).

surroundings, a way of behaving which was second nature to them in their own native environment. When Mrs. McIntyre holds out her hand for Mr. Guizac to greet her, he 'bobbed down from the waist and kissed it' (CS 195). They speak a different language, which makes communication rather difficult, at times painfully impossible, or so it seems. This gives rise to Mrs. Shortley's vividly imagined

'war of words, to see the Polish words and the English words coming at each other, stalking forward, not sentences, just words, gabble gabble gabble, flung out high and shrill and stalking forward and then grappling with each other. She saw the Polish words, dirty and all-knowing and unreformed, flinging mud on the clean English words until everything was equally dirty. She saw them all piled up in a room, all the dead dirty words, theirs and hers too, piled up like the naked bodies in the newsreel' (CS 209).

What affects the rest of the characters most is the fact that Mr. Guizac is 'Thrifty and energetic', that he is 'an expert mechanic, a carpenter, and a mason' (CS 201). His work ethic upsets the existing equilibrium on the farm and therefore he is felt to be a threat to everybody. '"He's extra and he's upset the balance around here"', says Mrs. McIntyre (CS 231).[6]

Mr. Guizac's behavior to the blacks also disturbs the existing order. He hands over the young farm hand Sulk to Mrs. McIntyre to be punished for his theft of a frying-size turkey, but leaves 'with a startled disappointed face' on hearing 'that all Negroes would steal' (CS 202). Even worse, prompted by family ties and true empathic commiseration he trespasses against the rules of racial segregation by suggesting that Sulk should marry his sixteen-year-old cousin from Poland. 'Mamma die, pappa die. She wait in camp. Three camp' (CS 223). This is so unheard of that Mrs. McIntyre for the first time is shaken, and with shocked wrath shouts, '"I cannot understand how a man who calls himself a Christian … could bring a poor innocent girl over here and marry her to something like that"' (CS 223).

Worst of all, the newcomers' Catholic background causes suspicion, fear and contempt. 'The Whore of Babylon' (CS 209) looms large in the story, personified in the figure of the priest, 'a longlegged black-

---

6   In a similar way The Misfit in O'Connor's story 'A Good Man Is Hard to Find' (CS 117-33) throws 'everything off balance' (CS 131).

suited old man with a white hat on and a collar that he wore backwards' (CS 195). Mr. Shortley sees him as the extended arm of the Pope
in Rome and Mrs. Shortley blames him for all that is happening. 'Mrs.
Shortley looked at the priest and was reminded that these people did
not have an advanced religion. There was no telling what all they believed since none of the foolishness had been reformed out of it. ...
They got the same religion as a thousand years ago. It could only be
the devil responsible for that' (CS 197-98; 206).

All these factors contribute to the impression that the Guizacs are
physically displaced people, and they are made aware of this by their
hosts. They move into a shack which is furnished in the most Spartan
way since 'they didn't have anything of their own, not a stick of furni-
ture or a sheet or a dish, and everything had had to be scraped together
out of things that Mrs. McIntyre couldn't use any more herself' (CS
196); yet their hosts think 'how lucky they were to escape from over
there and come to a place like this' (CS 196).[7]

The fact that Mr. Guizac has to work to earn his living and that he
has nowhere to go upsets the balance on the farm, so much so that all
the others are affected by it. First the Shortleys leave when Mrs. Shortley realizes the threat of being fired because of Mr. Guizac. This displacement affects Mrs. Shortley so deeply that she dies of a heart attack
in the car that carries them away from the farm. Later Mr. Shortley returns as a revenger, for he blames Mr. Guizac for his wife's sudden
death. '"I figure the Pole killed her ... She seen through him from the
first. She known he come from the devil"' (CS 227). Therefore 'it would
give him some satisfaction to see the Pole leave the place' (CS 227), to
see him displaced once again. He considers himself as an instrument of
God's wrath: 'Revenge is mine, saith the Lord' (CS 233).[8] Mr. Shortley
succeeds in displacing Mr. Guizac by arranging his violent death,
cleverly covered as a tractor accident, an accident the possibility of
which Mrs. Shortley had foreseen much earlier in the story: 'If don't
no terrible accident occur' (CS 205). However, Flannery O'Connor
makes it clear that Mrs. McIntyre, Mr. Shortley and the blacks, who all
witness the accident, share the conspirator's guilt in Mr. Guizac's death.
Mrs. McIntyre 'had felt her eyes and Mr. Sbortley's eyes and the

---

7   Here as in many other lines of the story we discover O'Connor's trademark, her
     covered attack upon the self-indulgent pharisaism of the hosts.
8   The quotation is from Deuteronomy 32:35 and Romans 12:19.

Negro's eyes come together in one look that froze them in collusion forever' (CS 234).

Mr. Guizac's violent death, his final 'displacement', results in the physical displacement of the entire Southern population of the farm: the same day 'Mr. Shortley left without notice to look for a new position and the Negro, Sulk, was taken with a sudden desire to see more of the world and set off for the southern part of the state. The old man Astor could not work without company' (CS 235).

Even Mrs. McIntyre, who had held on to the farm for thirty years and struggled for its continued existence ever since she had inherited it from her first husband, is now displaced. 'She saw that the place would be too much for her now ... and retired to live on what she had, while she tried to save her declining health' (CS 235).

At the end of the story we realize that physical displacement not only affects one group of people, the refugees or the officially displaced people, displacement affects also those who feel safely surrounded by their possessions. But physical displacement is not all, it is indicative of a much more comprehensive metaphysical displacement. At no point in the story is the reader left in doubt about the presence of a metaphysical dimension: angels and the devil are mentioned several times, and we recognize direct or inverted references to the Bible.

Mrs. Shortley has an apparently insurmountable physical presence: 'She stood on two tremendous legs, with the grand self-confidence of a mountain, and rose, up narrowing bulges of granite, to two icy blue points of light that pierced forward, surveying everything' (CS 194). But her eyes are capable of extraordinary outer and inner visions, which are triggered by the presence of Mr. Guizac. First she recalls 'a newsreel she had seen once' (CS 196) about the atrocities of Nazi concentration camps and which prompts her to an inversion of 'the golden rule' of doing to others as you would have them do toward you:[9] 'If they had come from where that kind of thing was done to them, who was to say they were not the kind that would also do it to others? The width and breadth of this question shook her' (CS 196). Her second vision concerns the blacks. Mrs. Shortley indulges in thinking of herself as their protectress against Mrs. McIntyre, who hopes that the Guizacs' arrival will 'put the fear of the Lord into those shiftless niggers' (CS 199). She

---

9   The rule is found in the book of Tobit 4:16. See also Mt 7:12 and Lk 6:31.

is fond of seeing herself as the blacks' friend: 'I hate to see niggers mis-
treated and run out. I have a heap of pity for niggers and poor folks' (CS
207). Yet while her unseeing eyes do not recognize the beauty of the
peacock's tail she has an inner vision of the displaced people's effect
upon the blacks: 'She was seeing the ten million billion of them pushing their way into new places over here and herself, a giant angel with
wings as wide as a house, telling the Negroes that they would have to
find another place' (CS 200).[10] As a person, according to her husband
gifted with 'omniscience', Mrs. Shortley's vision penetrates physical reality. When Mrs. McIntyre remarks enthusiastically about Mr. Guizac,
'"That man is my salvation!"' then 'Mrs. Shortley looked straight ahead
as if her vision penetrated the cane and hill and pierced through to the
other side. "I would suspicion salvation got from the devil," she said in
a slow detached way' (CS 203). She does not allow Mrs. McIntyre to
understand what she means by this, but O'Connor lets Mrs. Shortley
share her thoughts with the reader:

'She had never given much thought to the devil for she felt that religion was essentially for those people who didn't have the brains to
avoid evil without it. For people like herself, for people of gumption, it
was a social occasion providing the opportunity to sing; but if she had
ever given it much thought, she would have considered the devil the
head of it and God the hanger-on'. (CS 203-04)

Mrs. Shortley's most comprehensive vision is triggered by the presence of the priest, whom she regards as the root of all evil. This vision,
which is reminiscent of Old and New Testament vocational visions,
prompts her prophetic message: 'The children of wicked nations will be
butchered' (CS 210). What are we to make of Mrs. Shortley's visions?
On the surface she is a person thus gifted, but her prophecies do not reveal the voice of a good spirit; the voice seems distorted by selfishness.
Mrs. Shortley does not really care about the blacks, she has no understanding of the pain and the human tragedy behind the concentration
camp newsreel, she only sees the priest and Mr. Guizac as 'come to destroy' (CS 210). The arrival of the Guizacs changed her life: 'With the
coming of these displaced people, she was obliged to give new thought
to a good many things' (CS 204). Though not religious, she starts pray-
ing, '"God save me … from the stinking power of Satan!"' (CS 209) She
reads the Bible 'with a new attention' in an obvious attempt to seek jus-

10 Later in the story her husband refers to Mrs. Shortley as 'God's own angel' (CS 227).

tification for her negative vision of the displaced people. She feels a vocation to defend the existing order against all intruders from 'over there', she feels called to destroy the priest's influence, to destroy the Guizacs, to destroy 'the devil'. Just before Mrs. Shortley discovers that Mrs. McIntyre is going to fire her husband she reads the advertisement, 'I have been made regular by this marvellous discovery' (CS 211). Yet, on hearing that they will be discharged she does not recognize that the advertisement has gained a very concrete meaning for her. She has been made regular, all her giant strength is gone to smithereens, and what is left of energy she invests in collecting her things and her family and leaving the farm before daybreak. She is blind with defeat and anger: 'there was a peculiar lack of light in her icy blue eyes. All the vision in them might have been turned around, looking inside her' (CS 213). After the heart attack 'her fierce expression faded into a look of astonishment. ... One of her eyes drew near to the other and seemed to collapse quietly' (CS 213-14). Mrs. Shortley is not only displaced from the farm, she is displaced from life 'here'. As Flannery O'Connor formulates it: her family 'didn't know that she had had a great experience or ever been displaced in the world from all that belonged to her' (CS 214). O'Connor's last comment on Mrs. Shortley's displacement, 'her eyes like blue-painted glass, seemed to contemplate for the first time the tremendous frontiers of her true country' (CS 214) shows, I think, that Mrs. Shortley's physical displacement also has a metaphysical dimension. But what is Mrs. Shortley's true country? Is she allowed to 'see' her true country only after death? Was she at the moment of death, in which her body resembles the newsreel bodies, granted some kind of *visio beatifica?* Her eyes drawing near to each other could indicate that her vision *in extremis* is turned upon herself, that she is eternally fixed upon herself. O'Connor does not solve the question. The quality of her great experience is affected by the reading of the rest of the story.

Also Mr. Shortley's life changes through the meeting with Mr. Guizac. Before his wife's death a quiet man of few words, he returns after her death as a revenger, who speaks daggers to Mrs. McIntyre and the entire surrounding community: 'he was not going to wait with his mouth shut' (CS 233). He is a different person: 'The change in his face seemed to have come from the inside; he looked like a man who had gone for a long time without water' (CS 227). He finally succeeds in displacing Mr. Guizac once and for all, but he leaves as a man burdened with the guilt of murder. 'Mrs. McIntyre had changed since the Displaced Person had been working for her and Mrs. Shortley had observed the change very closely: she had begun to act like somebody who was getting rich secretly' (CS 207-08). Mrs. McIntyre is described as 'the one around here who holds all the strings together' (CS 217); for years she had struggled with 'shiftless niggers', with poor white trash. She had survived three husbands, although her first, the Judge, who had left her the impoverished farm, is still strongly present in his tombstone and in his many clichés which comment on the behavior of the people on the farm: 'One fellow's misery is the other fellow's gain' (CS 203, 208); 'The devil you know is better than the devil you don't' (CS 208, 217); 'We've seen them come and seen them go' (CS 214). Thus O'Connor creates the impression that Mrs. McIntyre never actually won the upper hand over her first husband. But her strength is underlined by the fact that she divorced her other two husbands, one to be put into an asylum, the other intoxicated somewhere in Florida. Therefore Mrs. McIntyre is respected as a person: 'nobody had put anything over on her yet' (CS 197). O'Connor describes her as 'a small black-hatted, black-smocked figure with an aging cherubic face, … as if she were equal to anything' (CS 224). Again it is Mr. Guizac who affects and finally shakes Mrs. McIntyre. Her changing attitude to the newcomer is indicative of this. Before he arrived she distanced herself from him by calling him 'Gobblehook'. In the period of her growing esteem for him she calls him Mr. Guizac, who saves 'her twenty dollars a month on repair bills alone' (CS 210). She regards him as her 'salvation', as 'a kind of miracle that she had seen happen and that she talked about but that she still didn't believe' (CS 219), and with satisfied affection she calls him 'the D.P.' (CS 214). But on noticing that he intends to bring his cousin over 'she was shaken'; now she calls him 'monster' and ends up talking about him derogatorily as the 'Pole'. Mrs. McIntyre tries to struggle against him, but feels her heart beating 'as if some interior violence had already been done to her' (CS 224). She tries to keep up defense mechanisms against his influence, but she feels weak. She pleads not guilty when the priest talks to her about her moral obligation to the Guizacs; nevertheless, she keeps putting off the date of their discharge from her place. But when Mr. Shortley denigrates Mr. Guizac even further, Mrs. McIntyre is so shaken that she felt 'she had a moral obligation to fire the Pole' (CS 233). Clad like a hangman she turns up on the site of his imminent violent death, yet she feels unable to fire him, frozen by paralysis.

Her meeting with Mr. Guizac and her conniving in his violent death displaced her completely: 'She felt she was in some foreign country where the people bent over the body were natives, and she watched like a stranger' (CS 235). Almost entirely disabled and isolated, Mrs. McIntyre lives through her private purgatory in that the only person who visits her is Father Flynn, who came to 'sit by the side of her bed and explain the doctrines of the Church' (CS 235).

This leaves us with the question: Who is this Mr. Guizac, who functions as a catalyst, who causes physical displacement as well as deeper insight in the people he encounters? Who is he, admired and hated, but finally rejected, as the 'abscess' his Polish name indicates?

As we have seen, the Shortleys regard him as an emissary of the devil; Mrs. McIntyre feels he is 'just one too many' (CS 231), who upsets the balance. The priest defends Mr. Guizac by directly comparing his situation to the one God's 'Only Begotten Son, Jesus Christ Our Lord' (CS 229) found himself in. Mrs. McIntyre's angry comment on this is revealing: 'as far as I am concerned, … Christ was just another D.P.' (CS 229). In this comparison I tend to see a key to an understanding of the deeper meaning of the story. The parallels between O'Connor's 'D.P.' and Jesus are obvious. He too was a displaced person, whom the pharisees regarded as a threat to their position, whom they had removed and killed. He also brought with him physical and metaphysical displacement. Mrs. McIntyre and the Shortleys had to give up their positions, their possessions, their 'place'. They experience this as being removed into a foreign country; yet it enables them to contemplate their 'true country'.

Flannery O'Connor succeeds in this story in a double way, I think. She addresses herself concretely to a social and political reality, the problem of refugees, of 'displaced' persons. In doing this, O'Connor also describes our post-lapsarian human situation: we are all displaced, we are in the world but not from the world, our eyes are held, but must be open to glimpses of 'our true country'.

Chapter 6

O'Connor's Presentation of Mystery and Evil

MYSTERY IN FLANNERY O'CONNOR AND EUDORA WELTY

It is the business of fiction to embody mystery through manners, ... The mystery [Henry James] was talking about is the mystery of our position on earth, and the manners are those conventions which, in the hands of the artist, reveal that central mystery. [The fiction writer is] concerned with ultimate mystery as we find it embodied in the concrete world of sense experience.

FLANNERY O'CONNOR (MM 124-25)

The sense of mystery in life we do well to be aware of. And, of course, I think we do try to suggest that mystery in writing a story, not through any direct or cheap way but by simply presenting the way things happen.

EUDORA WELTY[1]

In these two statements about the importance of mystery for their understanding of fiction, Eudora Welty and Flannery O'Connor seem to be largely in agreement. Welty talks about the 'sense of mystery in life' that is suggested in a story, O'Connor about 'the mystery of our position on earth' that is 'embodied in the concrete world of sense experience'. O'Connor seems to add a further epithet in that she expects fiction to 'reveal that *central* [my emphasis; or 'ultimate'] mystery'. I take this slight change of emphasis to be symptomatic for the two writers who knew and respected each other, though they were well aware of their differences. Welty told Jan Nordby Gretlund, 'I can't imagine ... three more different writers than Katherine Anne Porter, Flannery

---

1 Prenshaw, Peggy, ed., *Conversations With Eudora Welty*, New York, Washington Square Press, 1985. Hereafter in the text abbreviated as Welty Conversations.

O'Connor and myself' (Welty Conversations, 243-44). O'Connor also saw the differences: 'I am not one of the subtle sensitive writers like Eudora Welty' (HB 141). In another interview Welty was very generous in her tribute to O'Connor: 'Of course I think she is just tremendous. I think she was a fantastically gifted writer. I have enjoyed everything she has done. I love it'. Yet she also acknowledges that 'there are a lot of things I realize are a closed book to me in her work because of the Roman Catholic Church of which I'm ignorant' (Welty Conversations, 22). At one point even, when her brother was ill, Eudora Welty was gracious enough to invite Flannery O'Connor to replace her at the University of Chicago (HB 316). O'Connor herself counted Welty among the 'best Southern writers' (HB 98, 121) and in 1962, when they had been at a conference together, O'Connor wrote, 'I really liked Eudora Welty – no presence whatsoever, just a real nice woman' (HB 471). Yet later O'Connor became a little more apprehensive about some of Welty's work. She wrote to her friend 'A': 'You are right about the Welty story. It's the kind of story that the more you think about it the less satisfactory it gets' (HB 537).

Both writers differ widely in their upbringing and in their personal attitude to e.g. religious practice. Welty was baptized a Methodist but is [was] not a church-going person. Jan Nordby Gretlund concludes in his study *Eudora Welty's Aesthetics of Place*: 'Welty's own religious inclinations are singularly undramatic. In her fiction she does not offer religious hope'[2] and he quotes from Welty's autobiographical *One Writer's Beginnings*: 'I painlessly came to realize that the reverence I felt for the holiness of life is not ever likely to be entirely at home in organized religion' (33). But she adds: 'It was later, ... that the presence of holiness and mystery seemed, as far as my vision was able to see, to descend into the windows of Chartres, the stone peasant figures in the capitals of Autun ... in the shell of a church wall in Ireland still standing on a floor of sheep-cropped grass with no ceiling other than the changing sky. I'm grateful that, from my mother's example, I had found the base for this worship – that I had found a love of sitting and reading the Bible for myself and looking up things in it'.

O'Connor was a believing and active Roman Catholic, but she gratefully acknowledged: 'The fact that the South is the Bible Belt is in great

---

2 Gretlund, Jan Nordby, *Eudora Welty's Aesthetics of Place*, Columbia, University of South Carolina Press, 2nd edn, 1998, 332. Hereafter abbreviated as Aesthetics in the text.

measure responsible for its literary pre-eminence now. The Catholic novelist can learn a great deal from the Protestant South' (Magee, *Conversations with Flannery O'Connor*, 87). Both writers are as representatives of the fiction writing American South, well-known for their strong sense of place and concrete narrative detail in their short stories and novels. Critical response to their work has differed widely, but many critics seem to agree that a sense of mystery is almost absent in Welty, whereas most critics have focused on its presence in almost all of O'Connor's writings. It is my prime aim here to present Eudora Welty's and Flannery O'Connor's differing and parallel conceptions of mystery and to show the use of mystery in two of their fictions, i.e. in Welty's long novel *Losing Battles* (1970)[3] and in O'Connor's novelette 'The Lame Shall Enter First' (1962).

What Is 'Mystery?'

Before we enter into a discussion of the texts a few introductory remarks about the concept of 'mystery'. In Longman's *Dictionary of Contemporary English*, (London 1995, 939) 'Mystery' is defined as follows – according to frequency of usage: 1. Something 'impossible to understand or explain'. (2. is the verbal form of 1.) 3. 'a quality that makes someone or something strange, secret or difficult to explain'. 4. 'a quality that something has that cannot be explained in any practical or scientific way'. 5. 'a story about a murder'. The bulk of Welty's and O'Connor's work does not fit the category 'murder' story, though 'The Demonstrators' by Welty and 'A Good Man Is Hard to Find' by O'Connor would qualify. To both writers the idea of the Greek 'mystærion', that which is not said or seen, comes close to what they are doing in their stories. Flannery O'Connor leans in her treatment of the inexpressible or the inexplicable in the direction of St. Paul, who uses the term 'mystery' for a 'sacrament', in which an outward sign – say water in connection with baptism – is indicative of the inward and spiritual reality of grace, in the same sense as Jesus in the Incarnation is the physical sign of the spiritual godhead – 'and the word became flesh' [Jn 1:14] – i.e. the spiritual or internal reality is hidden behind the visible or the external, as Welty calls it, or in O'Connor's terminology, 'mystery' is revealed through 'manners'.

---

3   Welty, Eudora, *Losing Battles*, New York, Random House, 1970. Hereafter abbreviated as LB in the text.

Mystery as Understood by O'Connor and Welty

To Welty 'fiction isn't the place for philosophy', at least not 'when put in as philosophy' (Welty Conversations, 65). As Shelby Foote said in a conversation with Welty, I've never known Southerners do anything but tell stories',[4] they have – and these are Welty's own words – 'inherited, a narrative sense of human destiny' (Welty Conversations, 87). Or as O'Connor put it: 'When a Southerner wants to make a point, he tells a story; it's actually his way of reasoning and dealing with experience' (Magee, Conversations, 49). Particularly in connection with *Losing Battles*, which Welty wanted to be 'novel-as-drama' – with some 90% dialogue – (Welty Conversations, 273), in which all should 'be shown forth, brought forth, the way things are in a play, ... The thought, the feeling that is internal is shown as external' (Welty Conversations, 50; also 85, 208, 303). I see this as a clear authorial statement that the surface, the story, 'manners' is not all, that we have to look for something underlying, or in other words that *Losing Battles* is not only the story or the stories of a family's 'multi-front' battles but that they have a deeper dimension of 'mystery' as well. In 1972 Welty told Charles T. Bunting, 'The sense of mystery in life [, which 'is often lost sight of by reductive criticism'[5]] we do well to be aware of. And, of course, I think we do try to suggest that mystery in writing a story, not through any direct or cheap way but by simply presenting the way things happen' (Welty Conversations, 62). Mystery is omnipresent in the story, in the place and in the characters. In *The Eye of the Story* Welty states that all the arts are connected with place and 'all of them celebrate its mystery'.[6] 'From the dawn of man's imagination, place has enshrined the spirit' (Eye, 123). Against this background Cleo's teasing question in connection with Gloria's wedding gains greater depth: "'Do you all worship off in the woods somewhere?'" (LB 49) Welty also commented on mystery in relation to her characters: 'They know something else is out there. It's just an awareness of spaciousness and mystery of – really, of living, and that was just a kind of symbol of it, a disguise. I do feel that there are

---

4   Rubin,Lewis D., Growing up in the South – A Conversation', Louis D. Ruben, ed., *The American South*, Washington, USIS, 1991, 60.

5   Prenshaw, Peggy, ed., *Eudora Welty Critical Essays*. Jackson, University Press of Mississippi, 1979, 271, note 1. Hereafter abbreviated as Critical Essays in the text.

6   Welty, Eudora, *The Eye of the Story*, Vintage Books, NY, 1990, 119. Hereafter abbreviated as Eye in the text.

very mysterious things in life, and I would like just to suggest their presence – an awareness of them' (Welty Conversations, 342). In the same way Flannery O'Connor sees the depth dimension of the character as the novelist's central concern: 'A story always involves, in a dramatic way, the mystery of personality' (MM 90; also 198) and characters lean 'toward mystery and the unexpected' (MM 40). Welty and O'Connor seem to agree that: 'If the writer believes that our life is and will remain essentially mysterious, if he looks upon us as beings existing in a created order to whose laws we freely respond, then what he sees on the surface will be of interest to him only as he can go through it into an experience of mystery itself' (MM 41). Michael Kreyling has summed up Welty's presentation of deeper dimensions: She 'displays in the time- and place-bound particulars of Banner, Mississippi, the timeless combatants of a larger battle, one that can genuinely be termed cosmic. ... Welty views her people and their condition with the depth and breadth of the philosopher who sees the universal in each moment'.[7]

In *Losing Battles* Judge Moody quotes his old teacher Julia Mortimer, who wrote in her last letter, with clear overtones of the blessings of the Fall: 'The side that gets licked gets to the truth first' (LB 298). This statement is reminiscent of the title of O'Connor's story 'The Lame Shall Enter First', which again reminds us of the biblical promise 'The last shall be the first' (Mt 19:30).

Mystery in Losing Battles

Losing Battles has been interpreted in many different ways as the clash between the agrarian past of the Beecham-Renfro family and the future as taught by Julia Mortimer. Both Gossett and Heilman place central importance on young Jack as a biblical figure. 'For his family, Jack is a radiant innocent, a "blessed mortal", and a good Samaritan [Lk 10:30-37]. He is an incorruptible Prodigal Son [Lk 15:11-32] prodigally received with a feast and rejoicing and forgiving' (Critical Essays, 345; cf. 292). I think Welty uses the narrative elements from the stories of the Good Samaritan and the Prodigal Son quite to the point. This

---

7   Kreyling, Michael, *Eudora Welty's Achievement of Order*, Baton Rouge, Louisiana State University Press, 1980, 143-44; also 152. Hereafter abbreviated as Achievement in the text.

is just one instance, which proves Welty's ample knowledge of the Bible. Welty's answer to John Griffin Jones in a 1981 interview corroborates this: 'I love to read the Old Testament. The Old Testament has the best stories. The King James Version stays with you forever, rings and rings in your ears' (Critical Essays, 362). Little surprise therefore that a close reading of *Losing Battles* proves that Welty is permeated with the English of the Bible. I have discussed Welty's use of biblical language in my essay 'Conceptions of Mystery in Eudora Welty and Flannery O'Connor'.

Sin versus *Forgiveness*

One of the larger battles fought in *Losing Battles* is the recognition of evil and the individual's losing this battle in sin, and the necessity of forgiveness, which – on a different level – also is a form of losing. Welty accepts the presence of evil in her fiction, but does not seem to acknowledge 'sin'. In his first interview with Eudora Welty (1980) Gretlund suggested: 'You do not seem to be interested in the concept of "sin" or in the idea of "evil."' To which Welty answered: 'I am, though. Not in "sin" – not from a Roman Catholic point of view like Flannery O'Connor, because I am ignorant of that religion. But I do believe that there is "evil." I believe in the existence of "evil," or else your reaching for "good" could not mean anything. I do feel there is "evil" in the world and in people, very really and truly. I recognize its power and value. I do!' (Welty Conversations, 253) Therefore Gretlund concludes that 'Welty makes no attempt to hide the fact that inexplicable evil exists among [the Mississippi farmers]' (Aesthetics, 11) and that 'there is no attempt to explain away the tale of [Miss Lexie's] premeditated evil' (Aesthetics, 279), which is later atoned for because Miss Lexie is 'converted' to helping Jonas Hugg (LB 377). Yet Gretlund is not willing to accept, as some critics do, 'that only the presence of unexplained evil will give Welty's fiction its full depth' (Aesthetics, 276). I have little doubt that evil and sin loom large in *Losing Battles*. Awareness of sin is even present in little Elvie's skipping song: '"Yield not to temptation for yielding is sin"' (LB 137-38). Welty lets Judge Moody define "sin" as follows: '"I suppose it just aggravates whatever's already there, in human nature – the best and the worst, the strength and the weakness. ... And of course human nature is dynamite to start with"' (LB 319). In that sense almost all members of the reunion sense the presence of sin.

Uncle Curtis remembers Grandpa's last sermon in connection with the previous reunion: "'Oh, he thundered! He preached at us from Romans and sent us all home still quaking for our sins'" (LB 183). It is Uncle Nathan's mission, as his posters show, to raise consciousness of sin, which is a necessary presupposition for a growing understanding of forgiveness. Since the theme of Brother Bethune's reunion sermon is forgiveness, there is a progression from Grandpa's last threatening sermon based on St. Paul's letter to the Romans to Bethune's admonition, based on John the Baptist, to 'repent, for the kingdom of heaven is at hand' (Mt 3:2). He says, 'Forgiveness would suit us all better than anything in this lonesome old world' (LB 209, also 208-13 *passim*, 321, 372, 427, [Lk 24:47]). Forgiveness is so much in the air on the Beecham-Renfro farm that Judge Moody can say, "'Forgiving seems the besetting sin of this house'" (LB 319). In spite of all the sufferings the family has to endure, there is hope for a new beginning. Welty told Bunting, 'I wanted to show indomitability there. I don't feel it's a novel of despair at all. I feel it's more a novel of admiration for the human being, who can cope with any condition'. (Welty Conversations, 52) 'I wanted to take away everything and show them naked as human beings' (Welty Conversations, 54), a statement that is reminiscent of Lear's remark to Poor Tom [Edgar] in *King Lear* III,4,104 'Thou art the thing itself; unaccommodated man is no more but such a poor, bare, forked animal as thou art'. Danièle Pitavy-Souques concludes about Welty's description of the human condition that there is a 'depth of the tragedy of human relations behind the brilliant surface. ... Man's dignity and heroism is this endless fight against death and all forms of evil, which are forms of death' (Critical Essays, 267). 'Ultimately what Welty shows us is that man has within him the capabilities of being both godly and sinful' (Critical Essays, 366). But there is in *Losing Battles* an unmistakable movement from evil and sin to forgiveness and being good. One of the most striking images of this is the 'procession' of helpfulness and forgiveness with the school bus pulling the Buick and the van assisting with its brakes on their united way to Banner (LB 407).

I think it is important to notice Welty's carefully arranged similarity of tone at the end of Part III of the novel, which after Brother Bethune's sermon ends in forgiveness, and at the end of Part VI, where forgiveness is actually lived out by all parties involved. At the end of Part III the members of the family sing (LB 223):

> 'Gathering home! Gathering home!
> Never to sorrow more, never to roam!
> Gathering home! Gathering home!
> God's children are gathering home'.

There can be no question of the eschatological overtones of this hymn. Similarly at the end of the novel Jack sings (LB 436):

> 'Bringing in the sheaves,
> Bringing in the sheaves!
> We shall come rejoicing,
> Bringing in the sheaves!'

Both songs have the joyful overtones of returning home with a good harvest, but also returning home with life's harvest through 'The Gates of Beyond'.

Mystery in 'The Lame Shall Enter First'

In a characterization of her own work Flannery O'Connor said: 'To insure our sense of mystery, we need a sense of evil which sees the devil as a real spirit who must be made to name himself, and not simply to name himself as vague evil, but to name himself with his specific personality for every occasion. Literature, like virtue, does not thrive in an atmosphere where the devil is not recognized as existing both in himself and as a dramatic necessity for the writer' (MM 117, 168). She summed up her views in the well-known statements: 'My subject in fiction is the action of grace in territory largely held by the devil' (MM 178). 'Often the nature of grace can be made plain only by describing its absence' (MM 204). Preoccupation with the mysteries of evil and grace is clearly present in O'Connor's novelette 'The Lame Shall Enter First' (CS 445-82). The narrative structure of the story seems simple and straightforward: Mr. Sheppard – a consciously chosen eponymous name, because he wants to be a shepherd – is a recently widowed social worker and City Recreational Director, who lives with his ten-year-old son Norton, who is still deeply affected by the recent death of his mother. To show his concern for the poor, on Saturdays Sheppard works gratis in a boys' reformatory. Here he shows special concern for fourteen-year-old club-footed and highly intelligent (I.Q. 140) Rufus

Johnson, who when outside the reformatory lives with his religious grandfather, because his father is dead and his mother is in a penitentiary. His record is: 'senseless destruction, windows smashed, city trash boxes set afire, tires slashed' (CS 449). Sheppard's concern has a double function: he wants to educate his own spoiled son, Norton, who is 'selfish, unresponsive, greedy' (CS 449), by showing him his own affluence through the contrast with Rufus, who picks his food out of garbage cans. But more importantly, in his humanistic optimism he wants to 'save' Rufus Johnson by dragging him out of the morass in which he has ended through no fault of his own. [The characters here and their relations are reminiscent of the situation in O'Connor's novel *The Violent Bear It Away* (1955) with humanist Rayber and his son Bishop trying to 'save' Tarwater from his back-woods grandfather's Old Testament attitudes. Indeed, in a letter to John Hawkes, O'Connor called Rufus Johnson 'one of Tarwater's terrible cousins' (HB 456).] Sheppard spares neither efforts nor expenses to help Rufus and Norton: he buys both a microscope and a telescope to let the boys gain insight into the micro- and macrocosmic dimensions of the world. He also has a new shoe made for Rufus Johnson's clubfoot, which, however, he refuses to put on. Sheppard is truly an outstanding example of unselfish concern, it seems; though he is not quite perfect, because at a crucial point he does not trust Rufus Johnson's word of innocence and wrongly hands him over to the police.

This mistake only increases Rufus Johnson's aversion: he doesn't want any of Sheppard's concern. Right from the beginning Rufus hates Sheppard's do-gooding. Upon being asked who made him commit all those crimes, Rufus says: 'Satan. He has me in his power' (CS 450). Instead of accepting Sheppard's de-mythologized technological optimism – Sheppard foresees that Rufus will go to the moon one day – Rufus counters: 'When I die I'm going to hell' (CS 461). The mysteries of Satan and hell are concrete realities to the fundamentalist educated boy Rufus, but to Sheppard they are empty concepts, part of the bag of lies against which he wants to protect his son Norton. Rufus, the evil boy with a clubfoot as the devil's stigma, believes in Jesus and the Bible, so much so that, in imitation of the Prophet Ezekiel, he eats a page of the Bible. He sees through Sheppard's emptiness and tells Norton: 'He thinks he's Jesus Christ!' (CS 459) Later, when O'Connor describes him as 'a small black figure on the threshold of some dark apocalypse' Rufus twice spits into Sheppard's face: 'The devil has you in his power'

(CS 478). Finally, after his relapse into crime, Rufus returns to Sheppard with the police only 'to show up that big tin Jesus!' (CS 480), who is 'a dirty atheist' because he said 'there wasn't no hell' (CS 480). In a final attempt Sheppard tries to 'save' Rufus by saying: 'You're not evil, you're mortally confused. You don't have to make up for that foot' (CS 480). But Rufus retorts: 'I lie and steal because I'm good at it! My foot don't have a thing to do with it! The lame shall enter first [Mt 19:30]! The halt'll be gathered together. When I get ready to be saved, Jesus'll save me, not that lying stinking atheist' (CS 480).

Taken at face value, evil is victorious at the end of the story: Rufus is back on the path of crime, and Norton has committed suicide in an attempt to be united with his mother in heaven, which he believed to be at the far end of the telescope, where he thought to have seen his mother. Yet, what is more important, the mystery of evil, in the shape of Rufus, has functioned as a means of bringing Sheppard to the point of anagnorisis or self-recognition and possible conversion. Towards the end of the story he reflects: 'He had stuffed his own emptiness with good works like a glutton. He had ignored his own child to feed his vision of himself. He saw the clear-eyed Devil, the sounder of hearts, leering at him from the eyes of Johnson' (CS 481). He comes to recognize that he did 'the right deed for the wrong reason', as Eliot's Becket confesses in *Murder in the Cathedral*. In the final analysis, evil is not victorious at the end; on the contrary, Sheppard comes to realize his sin of pride and thus, I think, reaches a moment of grace.

Conclusion

In my discussion I hope to have shown that both Welty and O'Connor are writers who vividly describe manners, but also that they allow us to sense mysteries beyond manners. For both writers fiction deepens the mind's 'sense of mystery … by contact with reality, and its sense of reality … by contact with mystery' (MM 79), as O'Connor put it. The interplay between internal and external, between mystery and manners defines fiction as 'incarnational art' since it deals 'with all those concrete details of life that make actual the mystery of our position on earth' (MM 68). Though mystery is undeniably present in *Losing Battles*, Welty's novel, like her other work, has a more open-ended structure. In O'Connor's novelette as in her other work I sense a tendency towards closure and a final acceptance of an 'ultimate' mystery, which remains inexplicable: 'The fiction writer presents mystery *through* manners, grace *through* nature, but when he finishes there always has to be left over that sense of Mystery which cannot be accounted for by any human formula' (MM 153).

SHADES OF EVIL IN O'CONNOR AND WALKER PERCY

You're not evil, you're mortally confused.
SHEPPARD TO RUFUS JOHNSON IN O'CONNOR'S 'THE LAME SHALL ENTER
FIRST', CS 480.

In times like these when everyone is wonderful, what is needed is a quest for evil.
LANCELOT TO PERCIVAL IN PERCY'S NOVEL *LANCELOT*[8]

The works of Flannery O'Connor and Walker Percy (1916-1990) are saturated with the presence of evil in our modern world, which does not want to be aware of evil or at least not be made aware of the power of evil. I regard it as legitimate to consider the two authors under one heading because they have so many aspects in common: they belong to the same period – mid-20th century; they come from similar backgrounds: the American South, with its religious awareness; they knew each other and admired each other's works; and, based on their Catholic convictions, they struggled against all odds to show forth the mystery of evil – and grace – in what they considered an almost completely de-mythologized world. After a short discussion of their common understanding of evil I shall present two concrete examples of their treatment of the subject, i.e. O'Connor's short story 'The Lame Shall Enter First' (1962) and Percy's novel *Lancelot* (1977).

O'Connor and Percy corresponded with each other but in 1981 Percy stated in one of his interviews, 'I never really saw Flannery.'[9] After

---

8 Percy, Walker, *Lancelot,* New York, Avon Printing, 1978, 144. Hereafter abbreviated as L in the text.

9 Lawson, Lewis A. & Victor A. Kramer, eds, *Conversations With Walker Percy,* Jackson, University Press of Mississippi, 1985, 232. Hereafter abbreviated Percy Conversations in the text.

having read Percy's first published novel *The Moviegoer* (1961) O'Connor assessed it as being 'pretty good' (Percy Conversations, 192) and congratulated him on winning the National Book Award for it: 'I didn't think the judges would have that much sense but they surprised me' (HB 470). In a letter to her friend Caroline Gordon O'Connor talked about Percy as being 'our mutual admiration' (HB 238) and in March 1964 she called him 'our friend Walker' (CW 1204). Percy was much more explicit in his laudatory statements about O'Connor, whom he admired because 'she worked very hard' (Percy Conversations, 34), because she was dedicated to her art and because of her deep thinking.

In 1974 Percy told an interviewer: 'I would agree with Flannery O'Connor that my Catholicism is not only not a hindrance but a help in my work ... it's a way of seeing the world' (Percy Conversations, 88). But he was also critical: in 1981 he commented on O'Connor's expectation that the reader would realize the moment of grace in her stories: 'Well I'm not so sure you really see that. ... She sees her fiction in much more univocal, theological terms than I would see it. I think it works without that simple theological reading, and I think it had *better* work without that, or otherwise, if you have to share that feeling of grace with her to understand her fiction, I think she's in trouble' (Percy Conversations, 233).

Both authors cover common ground in that they see man as an actor on a stage with metaphysical depths, whereas their contemporaries tend to deny or at least neglect this depth dimension. O'Connor stated: 'I'm interested in the Old Adam' (Magee, Conversations, 98), man as fallen man, the feeling of which is particularly strong in the South, where 'we have had our Fall' (MM 59, 179), or as Percy formulated it where 'we lost the War' (Percy Conversations, 59) and where knowledge of the biblical view of man is still strong. 'We were doubly blessed, not only in our Fall, but in having means to interpret it' (MM 59). But Flannery O'Connor is also fully aware of the difficulty of getting this 'Christian vision across to an audience to whom it is meaningless' (Magee, ibid. 87). The only way for her to do this was to use 'extreme means' (Magee, ibid. 43; MM 58), among which her use of the grotesque, of 'freaks' was the most outstanding. 'Whenever I'm asked why Southern writers particularly have a penchant for writing about freaks, I say it is because we are still able to recognize one. To be able to recognize a freak, you have to have some conception of the whole man' (MM 44).

Similarly, Walker Percy conceived of man as 'somewhere between the angels and the beasts. He's a strange creature, whom both Thomas Aquinas and Marcel called *homo viator*, man the wayfarer' (Percy Conversations, 63-64; 13; 231). Man as 'a stranger' and 'a pilgrim' is the way in which Percy presented the human feeling of alienation in his books (Percy Conversations, 29). Man's loss of faith in God leads the wayfarer to existential 'despair' (Percy Conversations, 41), though all seems to be well on the surface. This existential paradox led Percy to the use of a 'harsh, satirical comic technique' similar to what he admired in Swift, Kafka and Heinrich Böll (Percy Conversations, 78). Since 'satire implies a norm' (Percy Conversations, 235) Percy used it to draw us back to an awareness of the norm. But like O'Connor he was aware that in his attempt to do this 'the language of religion, the very words themselves, are almost bankrupt. ... The themes have to be implicit rather than explicit' (Percy Conversations, 79).

The experience of *sin* plays an essential part in both authors' conception of man, but there is a modern trend to see sin only as a sickness, not as a dimension of evil. To O'Connor 'evil is not simply a problem to be solved, but a mystery to be endured' (MM 209). She was adamant and explicit about the presence of evil, more so than Percy. In a characterization of her own work she said: 'To insure our sense of mystery, we need a sense of evil which sees the devil as a real spirit who must be made to name himself, and not simply to name himself as vague evil, but to name himself with his specific personality for every occasion. Literature, like virtue, does not thrive in an atmosphere where the devil is not recognized as existing both in himself and as a dramatic necessity for the writer' (MM 117,168). In this context I think it is important to mention how concretely Flannery O'Connor saw the devil. In 1961 she had a discussion going with her fellow Catholic novelist John Hawkes about the devil. She wrote: 'My Devil has a name, a history and a definite plan. His name is Lucifer, he's a fallen angel, his sin is pride, and his aim is the destruction of the Divine plan. Now I judge that your Devil is co-equal to God, not his creature; that pride is his virtue, not his sin; and that his aim is not to destroy the Divine plan because there isn't any Divine plan to destroy' (HB 456). At the bottom of this, I sense the Enlightenment discussion of the origin of evil or the problem of 'theodicy': Did God create evil or is evil God's counterforce, independent of God's creation? Flannery O'Connor concluded: 'My subject in fiction is the action of grace in territory largely held by the devil' (MM 178). 'Often the nature of grace can be made plain only by describing its absence' (MM 204).

Preoccupation with evil is clearly present in the two examples from O'Connor and Percy's fictions which I have chosen for analysis: Rufus Johnson in 'The Lame Shall Enter First' (1962), as I have shown in my discussion of this story earlier in this chapter (pp. 115-17), and Lancelot Andrews Lamar in *Lancelot* (1977). Early on in his confession to Percival Lancelot touches upon the problem of evil. He says: 'Are you then one of the new breed who believe that Satan is only a category, the category of evil?' (L 21), that is, he thinks of Satan in a very concrete personified way, not just as a philosophical category. Like O'Connor's story, *Lancelot* seems straightforward and easy. Lancelot Andrews Lamar's more than a year's stay in a hospital – a mental home – is coming to an end. He was brought there because he had blown up his family mansion, Belle Isle, which had shortly before been restored by his wife Margot. Immediately before the explosion he had cut his wife's new lover's throat, and in the explosion he had killed his wife and Merlin, her former lover and father of the girl Siobhan, who Lancelot thought was his own daughter. Apart from the last two pages the entire novel is monologic, but the reader is always kept conscious of the presence of Percival, the interlocutor. Thus chapter two opens with: 'Come in, come in. Sit down. You still won't? I have a confession to make' (L 7). In the course of his confession to the priest, Percival, we get to know the reasons for Lancelot's deliberate choice of evil. Upon accidentally having detected the configuration of his 'daughter's' blood type Lancelot says, 'the worm of interest turned somewhere near the base of my spine' (L 29). His own and his wife Margot's blood types could never result in the daughter's type, therefore she can't be his. From that moment Lancelot follows the spy path of finding out about the truth, which gave him 'a curious sense of expectancy, a secret sweetness at the core of the dread' (L 41). For there is 'something worse than knowing the worst. It is not knowing' (L 139). Before the full truth dawns upon him, he discusses the question of evil with his interlocutor: 'How strange it is that a discovery like this, of evil, of a kinsman's dishonesty, a wife's infidelity, can shake you up, knock you out of your rut, be the occasion of a new way of looking at things' (L 53). In consequence of this Lancelot asks with St. Paul in Romans 3:8, 'Can good come from evil? Have you considered the possibility that one might undertake a search not for God but for evil?' (L 53)

Lancelot asks Percival to show him a pure example of sin, for that would almost make a believer of him, since it would be 'a new proof

of God's existence! If there is such a thing as sin, evil, a living malig-
nant force, there must be a God!' (L 54) So one could say that this is
Lancelot's sneaky attempt to prove the existence of God by deliber-
ately choosing – and he is proud of having 'the freedom to act on my
conviction' (L 166) – a quest for evil, for 'the Unholy Grail' (L 144).
'Evil', says Lancelot, 'is surely the clue to this age, the only quest appropriate to the age. For everything and everyone's either wonderful or
sick and nothing is evil' (L 145). In the course of his quest Lancelot
goes through different phases of getting a feel for evil. But after his
monstrous deeds of evil he asks, 'Why did I discover nothing at the
heart of evil? There was no "secret" after all, no discovery, no flicker-
ing interest, nothing at all, not even any evil' (L 274).

At the very end of the novel Lancelot agrees with Percival, who gives
a few monosyllabic answers: Yes and No, that 'One of us is wrong. It
will be your way [i.e. the quest for the Holy Grail or it will be my way
i.e. Lancelot's quest for the Unholy Grail]. *Yes*. All we can agree on is
that it will not be their way. Out there. *Yes*' (L 278-79). After his purga-
torial experience in the hospital and after having completed his confession, Lancelot intends to set out on a new beginning, a rebirth – sym-
bolically in Virginia – with the innocent Siobhan and with Anna, the
raped girl in the adjacent hospital room, now a 'new woman', with
whom Lancelot established a new system of communication by knock-
ing on the wall. The novel ends with the following words: 'I've finished.
Is there anything you wish to tell me before I leave? *Yes*' (L 279), but
Percival's answer is left open for the reader to interpret.

Lancelot can only recognize the evil done to him originally because
he still has an understanding of the norm or of what is good and what
is evil. But his experience of Margot's infidelity initiates him into the
pursuit of evil – with no satisfaction in the end. From this deadlock,
Lancelot wants to make a new start, and in that sense he is 'beyond
evil'. In that sense, to use Percy's own words, 'Lancelot is a conscious
combination of something quite positive and quite evil' (Percy Conversations, 208).

In both O'Connor's and Percy's narratives evil is present very concretely. Apart from a few short reflections on its essence, evil is not discussed abstractly, but dramatized in the actions of Rufus Johnson and
Lancelot. In both cases the protagonists are described as being increasingly possessed by the power of evil. There can be no doubt that both
authors are convinced of the destructive impact of evil. Both authors

attack our modern way of demythologizing evil, our attempts at explaining it in terms of social factors, of psychology or of illness and our way of getting around the question of evil by simply denying or at least ignoring its presence. Man is fallen, is affected by evil, and this will have to be taken into account. But it is also obvious in both texts that evil is not victorious in the end: evil is made to function as a means towards a new beginning.

List of Abbreviations

C   *Conversations with Flannery O'Connor*, Rosemary M. Magee, ed., Jackson, 1987.

CS   *Flannery O'Connor: The Complete Stories*, New York, 1971.

CW   *Flannery O'Connor: Collected Works*, Sally Fitzgerald, ed., New York, 1988.

Driggers   *The Manuscripts of Flannery O'Connor at Georgia College*, Stephen G. Driggers, ed., Athens, Georgia, 1989.

HB   *Flannery O'Connor: The Habit of Being*, Sally Fitzgerald, ed., New York, 1979.

MM   *Flannery O'Connor: Mystery and Manners*, Robert & Sally Fitzgerald, eds, New York, 1979.

Bibliography of Works Cited

Abrams, M.H., *A Glossary of Literary Terms*, New York Harcourt Brace, 6th edn 1993.

Alexander, Meena, 'The Postcolonial Imagination', interview with Prem Poddar. *Himal – South Asian*, vol. 14 no 1, (2001), 14-29.

Allen, William Rodney, 'The Cage of Matter: The World as Zoo in Flannery O'Connor's *Wise Blood*. *American Literature: A Journal of Literary History, Criticism, and Bibliography*, vol. 58 no 2 (1986) 256-70.

Als, Hilton, 'The Lonesome Place: Flannery O'Connor on race and religion in the unreconstructed South'. *The New Yorker*, January 29, 2001, 82-88.

Andersen, Flemming G & Lars Ole Sauerberg, eds, *Traditions and Innovations*, Odense, PEO, Odense University, 1994.

Angle, Kimberly Greene, 'Flannery O'Connor's Literary Art: Spiritual Portraits in Negative Space'. *The Flannery O'Connor Bulletin*, vol. 23, 1994-95, 158-174.

Archer, Emily, 'Naming in the Neighborhood of Being: O'Connor and Percy on Language'. *Studies in the Literary Imagination*, vol. 20 no 2 (1987) 97-108.

Asals, Frederick, *Flannery O'Connor: The Imagination of Extremity*, Athens, University of Georgia Press, 1982.

Asals, Frederick, '"Obediah," "Obadiah": *Guys and Dolls* and "Parker's Back"'. *The Flannery O'Connor Bulletin*, vol. 21, 1992, 37-42.

Asals, Frederick, 'Some Glimpses of Flannery O'Connor in the Canadian Landscape'. *The Flannery O'Connor Bulletin*, vol. 23, 1994-95, 83-90.

Baker, J. Robert, 'Flannery O'Connor's Four-Fold Method of Allegory'. *The Flannery O'Connor Bulletin*, vol. 21, 1992, 84-96

Balée, Susan, *Flannery O'Connor: Literary Prophet of the South*, New York, Chelsea House Publishers, 1995.

Baumgaertner, Jill P., *Flannery O'Connor: A Proper Scaring*, Wheaton, Illinois, Shaw, 1988.

Bawer, Bruce, 'Under the Aspect of Eternity: The Fiction of Flannery O'Connor', *The Aspect of Eternity*, Greywolf Press, Saint Paul, 1993, 309-20.

Beck, Christiane, 'Flannery O'Connor's Poetics of Space'. *Realist of Distances*, Karl-Heinz Westarp & Jan N. Grethlund, eds, Århus, Aarhus University Press, 1987, 136-46.

Ben Bassat, Hedda, 'Flannery O'Connor's Double Vision'. *Literature and Theology: An International Journal of Theory, Criticism and Culture*, vol. 11 no 2 (1997) 185-99.

Betts, Doris, 'Talking to Flannery'. Gordon, Sarah, ed., *Flannery O'Connor: In Celebration of Genius*, Athens, Ga.: Hill Street Press, 2000, 109-15.

Bible, The Holy, Rev. Standard Edition, New York, Collins, 1972.

Bieber, Christina, 'Called to the Beautiful: The Incarnational Art of Flannery O'Connor's *The Violent Bear It Away*'. *Xavier Review*, vol. 18 no 1 (1998) 44-62.

Bleikasten, André, 'The Heresy of Flannery O'Connor'. Melvin J. Friedman and B.L. Clark, eds, *Critical Essays on Flannery O'Connor*, Boston, G.K. Hall, 1985, 138-158.

Bloom, Harold, ed., *Flannery O'Connor*, New York, Chelsea House Publishers, 1986.

Bolton, Betsy, 'Placing violence, embodying grace: Flannery O'Connor's "Displaced Person"'. *Studies in Short Fiction*, vol. 34 no 1 (1997) 87-103.

Boren, Max Edelman, 'Flannery O'Connor, Laughter and the Word Made Flesh'. *Studies in American Fiction*, vol. 26 no 1 (1998) 115-28.

Brewer, Nadine, 'Christ, Satan, and Southern Prostestantism in O'Connor's Fiction'. *The Flannery O'Connor Bulletin*, vol. 14, 1985, 103-110.

Breit, Harvey, 'Galley Proof: A Good Man Is hard to Find' in Magee, *Conversations with Flannery O'Connor*, 5-10.

Brinkmeyer, Robert H., Jr., *The Art & Vision of Flannery O'Connor*, LSU Press, Baton Rouge, 1989.

Brown, Ashley, 'Flannery O'Connor: A Literary Memoir'. *Realist of Distances*, Karl-Heinz Westarp & Jan N. Gretlund, eds, Århus, Aarhus University Press, 1987, 18-29.

Brown, Preston M., *Flannery O'Connor*, Carbondale, Southern Illinois University Press, 1972.

Bruns, Jo, 'Struggling Against the Plaid: An Interview with Eudora Welty' in Prenshaw, *Conversations with Eudora Welty*, 330-43.

Budy, Andrea Hollander, 'An Enduring Chill'. Gordon, Sarah, ed., *Flannery O'Connor: In Celebration of Genius*, Athens, Ga.: Hill Street Press, 2000, 67-70.

Bunting, Charles T., '"The interior World": An Interview with Eudora Welty' in Prenshaw, *Conversations with Eudora Welty*, 43-69.

Burchett, George, *Memoirs of a Tattooist*, Peter Leighton, ed., London, 1958.

Burt, John, 'What you Can't Talk About'. Harold Bloom, ed. *Flannery O'Connor*, New York, Chelsea House Publishers, 1986, 127-34.

Carter, Thomas H., 'Rhetoric and Southern Landscapes'. *Accent* 15, 1955, 293-97.

Chappell, Fred, 'Vertigo'. Gordon, Sarah, ed., *Flannery O'Connor: In Celebration of Genius*, Athens, Ga.: Hill Street Press, 2000, 25-28.

Chardin, Pierre Teilhard de, *The Phenomenon of Man*, New York, Harper, 1959.

Chardin, Pierre Teilhard de, *The Divine Milieu*, New York, Harper, 1960.

Chardin, Pierre Teilhard de, *Letters from a Traveler*, New York, Harper, 1962.

Chow, Sung Gay, '"Strange and Alien Country": An Analysis of Landscape in Flannery O'Connor's *Wise Blood* and *The Violent Bear It Away*'. *The Flannery O'Connor Bulletin*, vol. 8, 1979, 35-44.

Cleary, Michael, 'Environmental Influences in Flannery O'Connor's Fiction'. *The Flannery O'Connor Bulletin*, vol. 8, 1979, 20-34.

Coles, Robert, *Flannery O'Connor's South*, Athens, The University of Georgia Press, 1993.

Comment Magazine, 'An Interview with Eudora Welty' in Prenshaw, *Conversations with Eudora Welty*, 19-28.

Corn, Alfred, ed., *Incarnation: Contemporary Writers on the New Testament*, Viking, NY, 1990.

Current-Garcia, Eugene & W.R. Patrick, eds, *What is the Short Story?* Glenview, Ill., Scott, Foresman and Comp., 1961, 2nd edn 1974.

Daretta, John L., 'From "The Geranium" to "Judgement Day": Retribution in the Fiction of Flannery O'Connor'. Loren Logsdon & Charles W. Mayer, eds, *Since Flannery O'Connor*, Macomb, Eastern Illinois University Press, 1987.

Davies, Horton, 'Anagogical Signs in Flannery O'Connor's Fiction'. *Thought*, vol. 55 (1980), 428-38.

Desmond, John F., *Risen Sons: Flannery O'Connor's Vision of History*, Athens, University of Georgia Press, 1987.

Desmond, John F., 'Signs of the Times: Lancelot and the Misfit'. *At the Crossroads: ethical and religious themes in the writings of Walker Percy*, Troy, N.Y., Whitston Publishing Company, 1997, 86-93.

Donahoo, Robert, 'Review of Karl-Heinz Westarp, *Flannery O'Connor: The Growing Craft*. *The Texas Review*, vol. XIV, nos 3&4, 1993, 90-91.

Donner, Robert, 'She Writes Powerful Fiction' in Magee, *Conversations with Flannery O'Connor*, 44-50.

Driggers, Stephen G., ed., *The Manuscripts of Flannery O'Connor at Georgia College*, Athens, The University of Georgia Press, 1989.

Driskell, Leon V. & Joan T. Brittain, *The Eternal Crossroads: The Art of Flannery O'Connor*, Lexington, The University Press of Kentucky, 1971.

Eggenschwiler, David, *The Christian Humanism of Flannery O'Connor*, Detroit, Wayne State University Press, 1972.

Eliot, T.S, 'Lancelot Andrewes'. *Selected Essays*, London, Faber&Faber, 1963, 341-53.

Eliot, T.S, *Murder in the Cathedral*, London, Faber&Faber, 1935.

Esprit, Winter 1959, 'A Symposium on the Short Story' in Magee, *Conversations with Flannery O'Connor*, 17-18.

Farmer, David, *Flannery O'Connor: A Descriptive Bibliography*, New York, Garland Publications, 1981.

Farnham, James S., 'Further Evidence for the Sources of "Parker's Back."' *The Flannery O'Connor Bulletin*, vol. 12, 1983, 114-16.

Feeley, Kathleen, *Flannery O'Connor: Voice of the Peacock*, New York, Fordham University Press, 1972.

Fickett, Harold, 'Why Do The Heathen Rage?' *The Catholic World Report*, April 1992, 56-59.

Fickett, Harold & Douglas R. Gilbert, *Flannery O'Connor: Images of Grace*, Grand Rapids, Michigan, W.B. Eerdmans Publishing Company, 1986.

Fitzgerald, Robert, 'The Countryside and the True Country'. Harold Bloom, ed., *Flannery O'Connor*, New York, Chelsea House Publishers, 1986, 19-30.

Fitzgerald, Sally, 'Degrees and Kinds'. *Realist of Distances*, Karl-Heinz Westarp & Jan Nordby Gretlund, eds, Århus, Aarhus University Press, 1987, 11-16.

Freeman, Mary Glenn, 'Flannery O'Connor and the Quality of Sight'. *The Flannery O'Connor Bulletin*, vol. 16, 1987, 26-33.

Friedmann, Melvin J. & Beverly Lyon, eds, *Critical Essays on Flannery O'Connor*, Boston, Mass., G.K. Hall, 1985.

Friedmann, Melvin J. & Lewis A. Lawson, eds, *The Added Dimension: The Art and Mind of Flannery O'Connor*, New York, Fordham University Press, 1977.

Gabler, Hans Walter et al., eds, James Joyce, *Ulysses*, New York, Garland Publications, 1984.

Gentry, Marshall Bruce, *Flannery O'Connor's Religion of the Grotesque*, Jackson, University Press of Mississippi, 1986.

Gentry, Marshall Bruce, 'O'Connor's Legacy in Stories by Joyce Carol Oates and Paula Sharp'. *The Flannery O'Connor Bulletin*, vol. 23. 1994-95, 44-60.

Gentry, Marshall Bruce, 'Review of Karl-Heinz Westarp, *Flannery O'Connor: The Growing Craft*'. *The Flannery O'Connor Bulletin*, vol. 22, 1993/94, 138-39.

Getz, Lorine M., *Flannery O'Connor, Literary Theologian*, The Edwin Mellen Press, Lewiston, NY, 1999.

Giannone, Richard, *Flannery O'Connor and the Mystery of Love*, Urbana, University of Illinois Press, 1989.

Giannone, Richard, *Flannery O'Connor, Hermit Novelist*, University of Illinois Press, Chicago, 2000.

Giannone, Richard, 'Warfare and Solitude: O'Connor's Prophet and the Word in the Desert'. Murphy, John J. et al. eds, *Flannery O'Connor and the Chris-*

tian Mystery, Salt Lake City, 1997, 161-89, also in idem *Hermit Novelist*, 144-69.

Gordon, Sarah, ed., *Flannery O'Connor: In Celebration of Genius*, Athens, Ga.: Hill Street Press, 2000.

Gordon, Sarah, 'Milledgeville: The Perils of Place as Text'. *The Flannery O'Connor Bulletin*, vol. 20, 1991, 73-87.

Gordon, Sarah, 'Notes From Afar: A Note on Structure in O'Connor's Narratives'. *The Flannery O'Connor Bulletin*, vol. 14, 1985, 80-87.

Gossett, Louise Y., '*Losing Battles:* Festival and Celebration'. Peggy W. Prenshaw, ed., *Eudora Welty Critical Essays*, Jackson, University Press of Mississippi, 1979, 341-50.

Graulich, Melody, '"They Ain't Nothing but Words": Flannery O'Connor's *Wise Blood*. *The Flannery O'Connor Bulletin*, vol. 7 (1978) 64-83.

Gray, Richard, *Writing the South: Ideas of an American Region*, Cambridge, Cambridge University Press, 1986.

Gretlund, Jan Nordby, 'A Neighborhood Voice: Eudora Welty's Sense of Place'. *Where? Place in Recent North American Fictions*, Karl Heinz Westarp, ed., Århus, Aarhus University Press, 1991, 99-107.

Gretlund, Jan Nordby, 'An Interview with Eudora Welty' in Prenshaw, *Conversations with Eudora Welty*, 235-55.

Gretlund, Jan Nordby, *Eudora Welty's Aesthetics of Place*, Columbia, University of South Carolina Press, 2nd edn 1998.

Gretlund, Jan Nordby, ed., Flannery O'Connor, 'An Exile in the East'. *The South Carolina Review*, vol. 11 no. 1, 1978, 3-21.

Gretlund, Jan Nordby, 'The Side of the Road: Flannery O'Connor's Social Sensibility'. *Realist of Distances*, Karl-Heinz Westarp & Jan N. Gretlund, eds, Århus, Aarhus University Press, 1987, 171-84.

Gretlund, Jan Nordby & Karl-Heinz Westarp, eds, *The Late Novels of Eudora Welty*, Columbia, University of South Carolina Press, 1998.

Gretlund, Jan Nordby & Karl-Heinz Westarp, eds, *Walker Percy: Novelist & Philosopher*, Jackson, University Press of Mississippi, 1991.

Grimshaw, James A., *Flannery O'Connor*, London, Greenwood Press, 1981.

Gross, Seymour, 'A Long Day's Living: The Angelic Ingenuities of *Losing Battles*' in Prenshaw, *Critical Essays*, 325-40.

Havird, David, 'The Saving Rape: Flannery O'Connor and Patriarchal Religion'. *The Mississippi Quarterly*, vol. 47, Winter 1993/94, no. 1,15-26.

Heilman, Robert B., '*Losing Battles* and Winning the War'. Peggy W. Prenshaw, ed., *Eudora Welty Critical Essays*, Jackson, University Press of Mississippi, 1979, 269-304.

Hendin, Josephine, *The World of Flannery O'Connor*, Indianapolis, Indiana University Press, 1970.

Hyman, Edgar, *Flannery O'Connor*, Minneapolis, University of Minnesota Press, 1966.

Jensen, Bo Green, 'De lamme skal komme først ind: om Flannery O'Connor'. *Afstandens Indsigt*, København, Borgen, 1985, 115-19.

Johansen, Ruthann Knechel, 'Flannery OConnor: The Artist As Trickster'. *The Flannery O'Connor Bulletin*, vol. 21, 1992, 119-39.

Johansen, Ruthann Knechel, *The Narrative Secret of Flannery O'Connor: The Trickster as Interpreter*, Tuscaloosa, University of Alabama Press, 1994.

Jones, A. Alling, 'Review of B. McKenzie, *Flannery O'Connor's Georgia*, (Athens, University of Georgia Press, 1980)'. *The Flannery O'Connor Bulletin*, vol. 9, 1980, 124-26.

Jones, John G., 'Eudora Welty' in Prenshaw, *Conversations with Eudora Welty*, 353-82

Joyce, James, *Stephen Hero*, Theodore Spencer, ed., New York, New Directions Paperback, 1963.

Kessler, Edward, *Flannery O'Connor and the Language of Apocalypse*, Princeton, Princeton University Press, 1986.

Kilcourse, George, '"Parker's Back": "Not Totally Congenial" Icons of Christ'. Murphy, John J. et al. eds, *Flannery O'Connor and the Christian Mystery*, Salt Lake City, 1997, 35-46.

Knauer, David J., 'The Incarnations of Flannery O'Connor – Review of Karl-Heinz Westarp, *Flannery O'Connor: The Growing Craft*'. *The Mississippi Quarterly*, vol. XLIX, no.1 (1995), 127-29.

Kranes, David, 'Space and Literature: Notes toward a Theory of Mapping'. *Where? Place in Recent North American Fictions*, Karl-Heinz Westarp, ed., Århus, Aarhus University Press, 1991, 11-21.

Kreyling, Michael, *Eudora Welty's Achievement of Order*, Baton Rouge, Louisiana State University Press, 1980.

Kreyling, Michael, *New Essays on* Wise Blood, Boston, Cambridge University Press, 1995.

Krings, H., 'Wort: I. Philosophisch', *Handbuch theologischer Grundbegriffe*, Band 4, DTV, München, 1962, 406-17.

Kuehl, Linda, 'The Art of Fiction XLVII: Eudora Welty' in Prenshaw, *Conversations with Eudora Welty*, 82-101.

Lawson, Lewis A. & Victor A. Kramer, eds, *Conversations with Walker Percy*, Jackson, University Press of Mississippi, 1985.

Lindroth, James R., 'A Consistency of Voice and Vision: O'Connor as Self-Critic'. *Religion and Literature*, vol. 16 no 2 (1984) 43-59.

Litz, Walton, ed., *Major American Short Stories*, Oxford, Oxford University Press, 1994.

Locke, John, *Essay Concerning Human Understanding* 1690, Book 3 chapter 11, 1.

Logsdon, Loren & Charles W. Mayer, eds, *Since Flannery O'Connor*, Macomb, Western Illinois University Press, 1985.

Longman's *Dictionary of Contemporary English*, 3rd. edn, London, 1995.

MacKethan, Lucinda H., 'Hogpens and Hallelujahs: The Function of the Image in Flannery O'Connor's Grotesque Comedies'. *Bucknell Review: A Scholarly Journal of Letters, Arts and Sciences*, vol. 26 no 2 (1982) 31-44.

MacKethan, Lucinda Hardwick, *The Dream of Arcady: Place and Time in Southern Literature*, Baton Rouge, LSU Press, 1980.

Magee, Rosemary M., ed., *Conversations with Flannery O'Connor*, Jackson, University Press of Mississippi, 1987.

Manning, Carol S., *With Ears Opening Like Morning Glories: Eudora Welty and the Love of Storytelling*, Westport, Conn. 1985.

Martin, Carter W., *The True Country: Themes in the Fiction of Flannery O'Connor*, Nashville, Vanderbilt University Press, 1969.

Martin, Carter W., '"The Meanest of Them Sparkled": Beauty and Landscape in Flannery O'Connor's Fiction'. *Realist of Distances*, Karl-Heinz Westarp & Jan Nordby Gretlund, eds, Århus, Aarhus University Press, 1987, 147-59.

Martin, Carter W., ed., *The Presence of Grace*, Athens, The University of Georgia Press, 1983.

May, Charles E., *The Short Story: The Reality of Artifice*, New York, Twayne Publishers, 1995.

May, John R., ed., 'Blue-Bleak Embers: The Letters of Flannery O'Connor and Youree Watson'. *New Orleans Review*, vol. 6, no 4, 336-56.

May, John R., *The Pruning Word: The Parables of Flannery O'Connor*, Notre Dame, University of Notre Dame Press, 1976.

May, John R., 'The Methodological Limits of Flannery O'Connor Critics'. *The Flannery O'Connor Bulletin*, vol. 15, 1986, 16-28.

McKenzie, Barbara, *Flannery O'Connor's Georgia*, Athens, University of Georgia Press, 1980.

McMullen, Joanne Halleran, 'The Verbal Structure of Infinity'. *Language and Literature*, vol. 21. (1996) 45-64 (In Writing Against God, chapter 6, 121-39)

McMullen, Joanne Halleran, *Writing Against God: Language as Message in the Literature of Flannery O'Connor*, Macon, Ga., Mercer University Press, 1996.

Mellard, James M., 'Review of Karl-Heinz Westarp, ed. *Where? Place in Recent North American Fiction*'. *The Mississippi Quarterly*, vol. 45, Spring 1992, no. 2, 200.

Messerli, Douglas, '"A Battle With Both Sides Using the Same Tactics": The Language of Time in *Losing Battles*' in Prenshaw, *Critical Essays*, 351-66.

Metcalf, John, 'The Curate's Egg'. *Zeitschrift der Gesellschaft für Kanada-Studien*, 1985 (5,1) vol. 8, 43-59.

Milroy, James, *The Language of Gerard Manley Hopkins*, André Deutsch, London 1977.

Montgomery, Marion, *Why Flannery O'Connor Stayed Home*, Sherwood Sugden, La Salle, Ill., 1981.

Muller, Gilbert H., *Nightmares and Visions*, Athens, University of Georgia Press, 1972.

Murphy, John J., ed., *Flannery O'Connor and the Christian Mystery*, Salt Lake City, Brigham Young University, 1997.

Nielsen, Erik, *Flannery O'Connors Romaner*, Odense, Odense Universitetsforlag, 1992.

Niederauer, George H., 'The Church Listens to Flannery O'Connor'. Murphy, John J. et al. eds, *Flannery O'Connor and the Christian Mystery*, Salt Lake City, 1997, 21-33.

Nisly, Paul W., 'The Mystery of Evil: Flannery O'Connor's Gothic Power'. *The Flannery O'Connor Bulletin*, vol. 11, 1982, 25-35.

Noyes, Tom, 'Review of Karl-Heinz Westarp, ed., *Flannery O'Connor: The Growing Craft*'. *American Studies International*, Oct. '97, vol. XXXV, no. 3, 97.

Oates, Joyce Carol, 'L'Imagination de Flannery O'Connor'. *Europe-Revue Littéraire Mensuelle*, 75.816 (1997) 43-47.

Oates, Joyce Carol, 'Where Are You Going, Where Have You Been?' Paul Lauter, ed., *The Heath Anthology of American Literature*, vol. 2, 3rd edn, Boston, Houghton Mifflin, 1998, 2178- 89.

O'Connor, Flannery, 'An Exile in the East', Jan Nordby Gretlund, ed., *The South Carolina Review*, vol. 11 no. 1, 1978, 3-21.

O'Connor, Flannery, *Collected Works*, Sally Fitzgerald, ed., New York, The Library of America, 1988.

O'Connor, Flannery, *The Complete Stories*, New York, Farrar, Straus & Giroux, 1971.

O'Connor, Flannery, *Conversations with Flannery O'Connor*, Rosemary M. Magee, ed., Jackson, University Press of Mississippi, 1987.

O'Connor, Flannery, *The Correspondence of Flannery O'Connor and the Brainard Cheneys*, Ralph C. Stephens, ed., Jackson, The University Press of Mississippi, 1986.

O'Connor, Flannery, *En god mand er svær at finde*, København, Grafisk Forlag, 1965.

O'Connor, Flannery, *Flannery O'Connor's Library: Resources of Being*, Arthur F. Kinney, ed., Athens, The University of Georgia Press, 1985.

O'Connor, Flannery, 'Getting Home'. Karl-Heinz Westarp, ed., *Flannery O'Connor: The Growing Craft*, Birmingham, Al., SUMMA Publications, 1993, 7-197.

O'Connor, Flannery, *The Habit of Being*, Sally Fitzgerald, ed., New York, Farrar, Straus & Giroux, 1979.

O'Connor, Flannery, 'The Letters of Flannery O'Connor and Youree Watson', May, John R., ed., *New Orleans Review,* vol. 6, no. 4, 336-56.

O'Connor, Flannery, *Mystery and Manners*, Robert and Sally Fitzgerald, eds, New York, Farrar, Straus & Giroux, 1969.

O'Connor, Flannery, *The Presence of Grace and Other Book Reviews by Flannery O'Connor*, Leo J. Zuber, ed., Athens, The University of Georgia Press, 1983.

O'Connor, Flannery, *Skæringspunkt og andre noveller*, København, Katolsk Forlag, 1984.

O'Connor, Flannery, *The Violent Bear It Away*, New York, Farrar, Straus & Giroux, 1960.

O'Connor, Flannery, *Wise Blood*, New York, Farrar, Straus & Giroux, 1962.

Olschner, Leonard M, 'Annotations on History and Society in Flannery O'Connor's "The Displaced Person."' *The Flannery O'Connor Bulletin*, vol. 16, 1987, 62-77.

Orvell, Miles, *Invisible Parade: The Fiction of Flannery O'Connor*, Temple University Press, 1972.

Paulson, Suzanne M., *Flannery O'Connor: A Study of the Short Fiction*, Boston, Twayne Publishers, 1988.

Percy, Walker, *Conversations With Walker Percy*, Lewis A. Lawson & Victor A. Kramer, eds, Jackson, University Press of Mississippi, 1985.

Percy, Walker, *Lancelot*, New York, Avon Printing, 1978.

Percy, Walker, *The Moviegoer*, New York, Alfred A. Knopf, 1961.

Pitavy-Souques, Danièle, 'Technique as Myth: The Structure of The Golden Apples', in Prenshaw, *Critical Essays*, 258-68.

Powers, Douglas, 'Flannery O'Connor's Treelines'. *The Flannery O'Connor Bulletin*, vol. 20, 1991, 54-60.

Prenshaw, Peggy W., ed., *Eudora Welty Critical Essays*, Jackson, University Press of Mississippi, 1979.

Prenshaw, Peggy W., ed., *Conversations With Eudora Welty*, New York, Washington Square Press, 1985.

Price, Reynolds, 'The Gospel According to Saint John'. Corn, Alfred, ed., *Incarnation: Contemporary Writers on the New Testament*, Viking, NY, 1990, 38-72.

Quinn, J.J., SJ, ed., *Flannery O'Connor: A Memorial*, Scranton, University of Scranton Press, 1995. (Reissue of *Esprit*'s special issue in 1964 in commemoration of Flannery O'Connor.)

Ragen, Brian Abel, *A Wreck on the Road to Damascus: Innocence, Guilt and Conversion in Flannery O'Connor*, New Orleans, Loyola University Press, 1989.

Rahner, Karl, 'Inkarnation'. Rahner, Karl et al. eds, *Sacramentum Mundi*, vol. 2, Herder, Freiburg 1968, 824-40.

Rath, Sura P. & Mary Neff Shaw, eds, *Flannery O'Connor: New Perspectives*, Athens, The University of Georiga Press, 1995.

Rath, Sura P., 'Ruby Turpin's Redemption: Thomistic Resolution in Flannery O'Connor's "Revelation."' *The Flannery O'Connor Bulletin*, vol. 19, 1990, 1-7.

Riffaterre, Michael, 'Hermeneutic Models'. *Poetry Today*, vol. 4.1 (1983) 7-16.

Rubin, Louis D., 'Growing up in the South – A Conversation'. Louis D. Rubin, ed., *The American South*, Washington, USIS, 1991, 59-90.

Scheffczyk, Leo, 'Wort Gottes'. Rahner, Karl et al. eds, *Sacramentum Mundi*, vol. 4, Herder, Freiburg 1968, 1402-13.

Schilling, Timothy P., 'Trying to see straight: Flannery O'Connor & the business of writing'. *Commonweal*, vol. 122 no 19 (1995) 14-16.

Schlier, H., 'Wort II. Biblisch'. *Handbuch theologischer Grundbegriffe*, Band 4, DTV, München, 1962, 417-39.

Schultz, Raphael, 'Sakrament'. Rahner, Karl et al. eds, *Sacramentum Mundi*, vol. 4, Herder, Freiburg 1968, 327-41.

Scott, R. Neil, 'UMI's Citations to Theses and Dissertations Related to Flannery O'Connor'. *The Flannery O'Connor Bulletin*, vol. 19, 1990, 77-99.

Sederberg, Nancy B., 'Flannery O'Connor's Spiritual Landscape: A Dual Sense of Nothing'. *The Flannery O'Connor Bulletin*, vol. 12, 1983, 17-34.

Selden, Raman, ed., *The Theory of Criticism*, Longman, London, 1988

Sharp, Paula, 'A Meeting on the Highway'. *The Imposter: Stories about Netta and Stanley*, New York, HarperCollins, 1991.

Shloss, Carol, 'Epiphany'. Bloom, Harold, ed., *Flannery O'Connor*, New York, Chelsea House Publishers, 1986, 65-80.

Shloss, Carol, O'Connor's *Dark Comedies: The Limits of Inference*, Baton Rouge, LSUPress, 1980.

Slattery, Dennis Patrick, 'Evil and the Negation of the Body: Flannery O'Connor's "Parker's Back."' *The Flannery O'Connor Bulletin*, vol. 17, 1988, 69-79.

Stephens, Martha, *The Questions of Flannery O'Connor*, Baton Rouge, LSUPress, 1973.

Stephens, Ralph C., ed., *The Correspondence of Flannery O'Connor and the Brainard Cheneys*, Jackson, University Press of Mississippi, 1986.

Streight, Irwin Howard, 'A Good Hypogram Is Not Hard to Find'. Murphy, John J. et al. eds, *Flannery O'Connor and the Christian Mystery*, Salt Lake City, 1997, 231-41.

Streight, Irwin Howard, *The Word Made Fiction: The Stories of Flannery O'Connor.* The Queen's University, Canada, 1995.

Trowbridge, Clinton W., 'The Comic Sense of Flannery O'Connor: Literalist of the Imagination'. *The Flannery O'Connor Bulletin*, vol. 12 (1983) 77-92.

Warren, Austin, 'Instress of Inscape'. Geoffrey H. Hartman, ed., *Hopkins*, Prentice-Hall, Englewood Cliffs, 1966, 168-77.

Wells, Joel, 'Off the Cuff' in Magee, *Conversations with Flannery O'Connor*, 85-90.

Welty, Eudora, *Conversations With Eudora Welty*, Peggy Prenshaw, ed., New York, Washington Square Press, 1985.

Welty, Eudora, 'Flannery O'Connor'. *Esprit, Journal of Thought and Opinion*, vol. 8, no.1, Winter 1964, 49.

Welty, Eudora, *Losing Battles*, New York, Random House, 1970.

Welty, Eudora, *One Writer's Beginnings*, Cambridge, Mass., Harvard University Press, 1994.

Welty, Eudora, 'Place in Fiction'. *The Eye of the Story*, Vintage Books, New York, 1990, 116-33.

Welty, Eudora, *The Eye of the Story*, Vintage Books, NY, 1990.

Welty, Eudora, 'The Reading and Writing of Short Stories'. Current-Garcia, Eugene & W.R. Patrick, eds, *What is the Short Story?* Glenview, Ill., Scott, Foresman and Comp., 1961, 108-15.

Westarp, Karl-Heinz, 'Beyond Loss: Eudora Welty's *Losing Battles*' Jan Nordby Gretlund & Karl-Heinz Westarp, eds, *The Late Novels of Eudora Welty*, Columbia, University of South Carolina Press, 1998, 56-66.

Westarp, Karl-Heinz, ed., Flannery O'Connor, 'Getting Home'. Karl-Heinz Westarp, ed., *Flannery O'Connor: The Growing Craft*, Birmingham, Al., SUMMA Publications, 1993, 7-197.

Westarp, Karl-Heinz, 'Message to the Lost Self: Percy's Analysis of the Human Situation'. *Renascence*, vol. XLIV, No. 3, 1992, 216-24.

Westarp, Karl-Heinz and Jan Nordby Gretlund, eds, *Realist of Distances: Flannery O'Connor Revisited*, Århus, Aarhus University Press, 1987.

Westarp, Karl-Heinz, ed., *Where? Place in Recent North American Fiction*, Århus, Aarhus Universitetsforlag, 1991.

Weston, Ruth D., *Gothic Traditions and Narrative Techniques in the Fiction of Eudora Welty*, Baton Rouge 1994.

Whitt, Margaret Earley, *Flannery O'Connor*, University of South Carolina Press, Columbia, 2nd edn, 1997.

Williams, Miller, 'Remembering Flannery O'Connor'. Gordon, Sarah, ed., *Flannery O'Connor: In Celebration of Genius*, Athens, Ga.: Hill Street Press, 2000, 1-4.

Wood, Ralph C., 'The Heterodoxy of Flannery O'Connor's Book Reviews'. *The Flannery O'Connor Bulletin*, vol. 5, 1976, 3-29.

Wray, Virginia F., '"An Afternoon in the Woods": Flannery O'Connor's Discovery of Theme'. *The Flannery O'Connor Bulletin*, vol. 20, 1991, 45-53.

Zacharasiewics, Waldemar, 'From the State to the Strait of Georgia: Aspects of the Response by Some of Flannery O'Connor's Creative Readers'. *Realist of Distances*, Karl-Heinz Westarp & Jan Nordby Gretlund, eds, Århus, Aarhus University Press, 1987, 171-84.

List of the Author's Previously Published Material on O'Connor

'"Judgement Day': The Published Text *versus* Flannery O'Connor's Final Version', *The Flannery O'Connor Bulletin*, vol. 11 (1982), 108-22.

'"Parker's Back": A Curious Crux Concerning Its Sources', *The Flannery O'Connor Bulletin*, vol. 11 (1982), 1-9.

'Teilhard de Chardin's Impact on Flannery O'Connor: A Reading of "Parker's Back"', *The Flannery O'Connor Bulletin*, vol. 12 (1983), 93-113.

'Indledning' to Flannery O'Connor: *Skæringspunkt og andre noveller*, København, 1984, 7-11.

'Flannery O'Connor's Development: An Analysis of the Judgement-Day Material', Karl-Heinz Westarp & Jan Nordby Gretlund, eds, *Realist of Distances: Flannery O'Connor Revisited*, Aarhus 1987, 46-54.

'Flannery O'Connor's Displaced Persons', Karl-Heinz Westarp, ed., *Where? Place in Recent North American Fictions*, Aarhus, 1991, 89-98.

'Erik Nielsen, *Flannery O'Connors Romaner*', *The Flannery O'Connor Bulletin*, vol. 21 (1992), 140-43.

Flannery O'Connor: The Growing Craft, A Synoptic Variorum Edition of 'The Geranium', 'An Exile in the East', 'Getting Home' and 'Judgement Day', SUMMA Publications, Birmingham, Alabama, 1993.

'Shades of Evil in the Fictions of Flannery O'Connor and Walker Percy', Flemming G. Andersen & L.O. Sauerberg, eds, *Traditions and Innovations*, Odense, 1994, 373-80.

'Conceptions of Mystery in Eudora Welty and Flannery O'Connor', Karl-Heinz Westarp, ed., *The Literary Man*, Aarhus, 1996, 164-79.

'Precision and Depth in Flannery O'Connor's Short Stories', *Rationality and the Liberal Spirit*, Centenary College of Louisiana, Shreveport, 1997, 149-61.

'Flannery O'Connor's Translucent Settings', *American Studies in Scandinavia*, vol. 31, no 2 (1999), 31-41.

Index

Listed are all names given in texts and notes.

References to Flannery O'Connor's works are listed alphabetically.

Major themes are listed as subdivisions under the entry of O'Connor, Flannery.